I'VE TASTED MY BLOOD

—the TROUT POND—

I. Rosenblatt Jan 2/75—

MILTON ACORN

I'VE
TASTED
MY BLOOD

POEMS 1956 TO 1968

SELECTED BY AL PURDY

Steel Rail Educational Publishing
Toronto Canada
1978

Steel Rail Educational Publishing

Steel Rail Educational Publishing is incorporated as a corporation without share capital and is directed by the Steel Rail Collective.

The aim of Steel Rail is to encourage and facilitate research into a greater understanding of Canadian society and the role of the citizen in our society. Steel Rail's policy is to strive for production of material which will not only encourage people to participate in the struggle for liberation, by providing pride and confidence in our own achievements and history, but which will also give us a proud and new direction for the future.

Canadian Cataloguing in Publication Data

Acorn, Milton, 1923-
  I've tasted my blood

ISBN 0-88791-010-6 pa.

I. Purdy, Alfred., 1918-   II. Title.

PS8501.C64194 1977   C811'.5'4   C77-001538-7
PR9199.3.A18I94 1977

I've Tasted My Blood
  1st printing ....1969 The Ryerson Press
  2nd printing ....   McGraw-Hill Ryerson Ltd.
  3rd printing ....   McGraw-Hill Ryerson Ltd.
  4th printing ....1978 Steel Rail Educational Publishing

*"I am a thousandth generation
Canadian and I write poetry
to entertain. The important
thing about poetry is
honesty. I am careful to
express what I want to say
clearly, to use a secondary
theme running through the
images, to make my work
beautiful if not compre-
hensible.*

*"I have called myself many
things; but I guess the one
that sticks is 'Revolutionary
Poet'—that is revolutionary
in the political sense,
not the poetic sense."*

Also by Milton Acorn
   In Love and Anger (1956)
   Against a League of Liars (1960)
   Jawbreakers (1963)
   58 Poems by Milton Acorn (1963)
      a Special edition of "Fiddlehead"
   More Poems for People (1972)
   The Island Means Minago (1975)
   Jackpine Sonnets (1977)

I've Tasted My Blood ISBN 0-88791-010-6
Milton Acorn

Steel Rail Educational Publishing
71 Bathurst Street
Toronto, Ontario
M5W 1X6

Printed and bound in Canada by Webcom Limited

This book is published with the assistance of a grant from the
Ontario Arts Council.

ACKNOWLEDGMENTS

The following poems appeared first in *Canadian Forum*: Death Poem, Saint-Henri Spring, Monument, Joe Dying, Poem Poem, Rebuttals, The Machine Gunner, Restaurant Scene, In Addition, At El Cortijo, Problem, The Trout Pond, The Tapeworm, Ashaye Dancing, "Callum", Two Players, The Idea, On Saint-Urbain Street, Nature, I Shout Love, Idyl, You Growing, Chess, Request, Bright Moon, Scream a Cream Cone, Live with Me on Earth Under the Invisible Daylight Moon, Poem Written in a One-Tree Forest, and A Worried but Easy Habit. Pastoral, Parting, I Spun You Out, Poem, The One-eyed Seaman, Girl, House, Blackfish Poem, Offshore Breeze, Lee Side in a Gale, The Schooner, Summer: Downtown Montreal, Why a Carpenter Wears His Watch Inside the Wrist, Boy Fishing at a Pier, More Intricate, Haiku, Robert, The Damnation Machine, Hear with the Wind Still, Charlottetown Harbor, Old Property, Islanders, July Creatures, The Fights, Canadian Winter 1960/61, and Poem with Fat Cats in the Background were in *Fiddlehead*. The Cigarette Machine, The King Rains, Ghostly Story, and Words Said Sitting on a Rock were in *Prism*. Autumn an Era, The Tolerant Philistine, and Knowing I Live in a Dark Age appeared in *Delta*; Of Martyrs, and The Hands, in *New Frontiers*. An Untidy Room, Rooming House, Detail of a Cityscape, and Poem for a Singer were in *Prometheus*. Where Is Che Guevara? appeared in *Progressive Worker*; Tears the Dew of Beauty's Mourning, and Tonguecut Prints of a Child Mouth as Birds, in *West Coast Review*. Poem, Poem for Sydney, In Victory Square, The Natural History of Elephants were in *Blew Ointment*. I've Tasted My Blood, Encounter, In Memory of Tommy an Orphan, Inland Gull, Images for the Season, November Beach, Sky's Poem for Christmas, A Bastard's Story, "Murder", Lifeblood Soliloquy, Girl at a Crossroads, Only a Recession, Week in French Canada, View from a Time Machine, January Sparrow are from *Jawbreakers* (Contact Press 1963). In *Against a League of Liars* (Hawkeshead Press 1961) were: I Will Arise and Go Now, Cynicism, Winter Boarders, Death's Incarnation, Picasso's Seated Athlete with Child, Annie's Son, Letter to My Redheaded Son, More Blessed. Libertad, Belle, The Island, Mike, In the Thief's Mindseye appeared for the first time in *The Brain's the Target* (The Ryerson Press 1960). Two poems are from *In Love and Anger*, privately printed in 1956: November, and My Love a Fierce Altruist.

Also thanks to The First Floor Club, The Bohemian Embassy, La Place, The Third Eye, The Advance Mattress and other coffee houses where many of these poems developed in participation with the audience. Especial thanks to Don Cullen and John Robert Colombo for arranging such readings.
                                                                    M.A.

The following poems were written for love,
especially love of the Working People
and the Youth; and for the poets Al Purdy,
Dorothy Livesay and F. R. Scott. As Dylan Thomas
said, "I'd be a damn fool if they weren't."

La vérité c'est que j'aimais
Et la vérité c'est que j'aime
De jour en jour l'amour me prend première. . . .

Paul Eluard

The very truth is that I've loved
And the very truth is that I love still
Each day
        love
                is my first thought

You are invited to salute
Milton Acorn
the people's poet
at Grossman's Tavern
79 Spadina Avenue, Toronto
on Saturday, May 16th
from 7:30 p.m. till midnight
for the presentation of
The Canadian Poet's Award
created this year to honour
Milton Acorn's book
I'VE TASTED MY BLOOD
cash bar and food

Left to right: Bryan McCarthy, Irving Layton, Avi Boxer, Niema Ash, Eli Mandel and Margaret Atwood honouring Milton Acorn with the title of "The People's Poet" in recognition of his book I've Tasted My Blood (Montreal Star Photo courtesy Metropolitan Toronto Library Board)

Preface to the Second Edition of
I've Tasted My Blood

It's a proud thing for Canada when a poet can truthfully say that a book of his is reprinted by popular demand. Also, since I'VE TASTED MY BLOOD is an historic document the STEEL RAIL COLLECTIVE has agreed that it must be reprinted exactly as it was before, with footnotes to note the few misprints, and the odd poem or verse which the author would no longer stand behind.

If things were perfect in this imperfect world, I'VE TASTED MY BLOOD would consist of two volumes. The first, consisting of the first half of this opus, would be JAWBREAKERS: the second a volume I would have named POEMS COMMITTED . . . the dividing line between these two sections being roughly where the two short stories are inserted.

A few poems remain misplaced. *I'D LIKE TO MARK MYSELF, THE GOLDENRODS ARE COMING UP,* and *ROOMING HOUSE*; included in the first section, should be in the second. The poem entitled POEM, on page 115 of the second section, should be in the first. The second section is at once more speculative and more political than the first.

After I'd written JAWBREAKERS, I considered I'd said what I had to say; and my poetic career was over. Fate intervened with a number of hard knocks, making me again useless for anything but writing poetry, and my odyssey of words went on. Finally, through the intervention of Al Purdy I'VE TASTED MY BLOOD appeared under the sigma of the Ryerson Press. Shortly after that Ryerson Press elected to 'sell my contract' to McGraw-Hill, later McGraw-Hill Ryerson. I and several others stood like a stone wall against that bit of quasi-legal dealing. Purdy even withdrew a manuscript already in progress.

Meantime several other things had happened. When the Governor-Generals Medal had been instituted by the Canadian Authors Association, its annual awardment had been managed on the whole fairly. After it was taken over by the Canada Council it had become a political football. In one year the prose award had been given to Igor Gouzenko for a book which still graces the remainder shelves. I'VE TASTED MY BLOOD was the odds-on favorite for the G.G. (as it is known) in 1969 . . . but the award went to a couple of others. At least one American without Canadian citizenship was on the award committee that year.

The result was a stunning rally of the poets. An act of rebellion such as is rarely scene in literary circles. In 1970, in a raucus assembly at Grossman's Tavern, I was awarded the as-yet unique Canadian Poets Award—along with a cheque for $1,000.00. The Canada Council generously chipped in with another $5,000.00 (not called part of the same award) and poetry for the first time in decades made a national news story.

On the reverse side of the medal, put there by Joe Rosenblatt and Stephanie Nynnich, were inscribed the words THE PEOPLES POET, which has remained my nomme-de-guerre.

When this book came out in 1969, I immediately went down to Ryerson Press and took fifty on credit. Within a week I'd sold that fifty and was down again, paid up my bill and took another fifty. By the third time I was greeted on my way out by a whole line of Ryerson office staffers come to cheer and jeer me on, and absolutely stunned at this spectacle of a poet flogging his own books. When I told them the royalty plus the much larger dealer's commission looked a hell of a lot better than just the royalty; they were even more amused.

When Domitian, son of the emperor Vespasian, objected to the lavatory tax as undignified; Vespasian handed him a coin from the proceeds, asking him: "Smell it. Does it stink?" To tell the truth I've got no memory of where and to whom I sold those books . . . I've absolutely blanked it out. I'm not the first nor will I be the last man who has had to earn his living by unpleasant means. True, I receive a pension for an injury incurred on active service. There are many others whom the Pensions Commission considers 100% percent disabled who manage to be useful citizens just the same. The refusal of the government to increase the pension this year, though it affects me little, is a dastardly repudiation of a fair debt.

Thanks go to Al Purdy for giving over his share of the royalty on this book, for a paltry consideration. Purdy's magnificent introduction to the first edition is included. Some thought the jovial mood of Purdy's spiel inappropriate. I've never taken myself so seriously as others would wish me to.

Milton Acorn
Jan. 26, 1978

INTRODUCTION

✦1

"Irving Layton sent me," the big red-faced man said, shuffling his feet at the apartment door. "He told me you wrote plays for CBC and could give me some tips—"

That was the first time I met Milton Acorn, a hot summer evening in Montreal in 1958, hot inside and out. We talked poems until early morning, disagreeing violently about almost everything, but seemed to get along well anyway. Drama was scarcely mentioned in that discussion: besides I wasn't really much of a playwright: I had to write a dozen plays before I got one accepted by CBC.

For the next few years I saw quite a bit of Milton Acorn. He was a carpenter by trade, but had decided to give it up and be a writer, just like that. I went along when he sold his expensive-looking tools at a shop on St. Antoine St. Talk about burning your bridges! But Milton had made up his mind to sell those tools, and couldn't be convinced to wait until he made some money writing. And as it turns out, I think he was right.

Montreal at that time was a nest of poets—including Louis Dudek, Irving Layton, Frank Scott, Miriam Waddington, Alan Pearson, Bryan McCarthy, Eldon Grier, Ron Everson, and several others. I was there myself because I'd sold in Vancouver the first play I ever wrote and decided that I was a writer of genius and all I had to do was turn out the stuff like sausage, Montreal being a good place to make sausages and drink beer. Acorn was from Prince Edward Island, thirty-four years old, and had been in the army during the early years of the war.

During that winter of 1956-57 Acorn and myself wrote poems and plays, did a great deal of talking, and went to the occasional party at Irving Layton's or Louis Dudek's. Milton had published a small book of poems at his own expense the year before I met him, called "In Love and Anger." I was not impressed with this book, for the poems were highly metrical and, I thought, pretty sentimental. I felt I was an authority on sentimentality, something I may never escape.

But in 1957 Milton was writing excellent short lyrics, in fact much better poems than mine, which I didn't realize then. He had a room on St. Antoine St., a place where you had to wade knee-deep thru poems, wastepaper and books. The only free space in the room was above your waist.

In 1957 I used the proceeds from two play-sales to CBC to buy a pile of used lumber and make the down payment on a lot at Roblin Lake, near Ameliasburg, Ont. My wife and I built a cottage there, and settled down to a life of rural discomfort where you had to cluster five coal-oil lamps to read a book at night. I still pretended to be a writer, and my wife had made up her mind that if I could get away without working she could too. We watched each other for months to see who would weaken first. In 1959 both of us gave way at once, and we went back to Montreal to get jobs rather than endure further starvation.

Milton was still there, living on Sanguinet and later on St. Urbain St. I don't know what he was doing for money; most of the time he didn't have any. After I got a job at a mattress factory on St. Germain in Montreal East he came and stayed at our apartment, sometimes for a day or two and sometimes for a couple of weeks. We started a "little" magazine, "Moment," around that time. Milt liberated a used mimeograph machine from somewhere (I think it belonged to the C.P.), and we turned out the magazine on the floor of our Maplewood apartment.

As I've said, Acorn and I used to disagree on practically everything. I'm not sure how such disagreement was possible between two people who remained friends. But Milton took advantage of me: he read all my books for ammunition, and fired the arguments back at me faster than I could read them myself. Once he read a four-volume set of Sigmund Freud (free gift from a book club) from cover to cover before I had even opened it, and was full of psychological information to confound me with when I came home from work. I had to read at frantic speed to catch up and protect myself in the semantic clinches.

In 1960 I quit my job making box springs for other men's playgrounds, and went back to the cottage at Roblin Lake. Milton came with me, my wife remaining in Montreal to keep the away fires burning. It was early March at Roblin Lake and cold. There was no fuel for the wood stove, but plenty of scrap lumber I'd scrounged from the C.P.R. Milt and I cut it up with a handsaw and frozen hands. And continued our long argument. Later I wrote a poem about that time, one that seems to tell more than I can say in prose. It's the closest we'll come to publishing the book we wanted to do together, this poem of mine in his book.

HOUSE GUEST

For two months we quarreled over socialism   poetry   how to
     boil water
doing the dishes   carpentry   Russian steel production figures
     and whether
you could believe them and whether Toronto Maple Leafs would
     take it all
that year and maybe hockey was rather like a good jazz combo
never knowing what came next

Listening
how the new house made with salvaged old lumber
bent a little in the wind and dreamt of the trees it came from
the time it was travelling thru
and the world of snow moving all night in its blowing sleep
while we discussed ultimate responsibility for a pile of dirty dishes
Jews in the Negev   the Bible as mythic literature   Peking Man
and in early morning looking outside to see the pink shapes of wind
printed on snow and a red sun tumbling upward almost touching
        the house
and fretwork tracks of rabbits outside where the window light had
        lain
last night an audience
watching in wonderment the odd human argument
that uses words instead of teeth
and got bored and went away

Of course there was wild grape wine and a stove full of Douglas fir
(railway salvage) and lake ice cracking its knuckles in hard Ontario
        weather
and working with saw and hammer at the house all winter
        afternoon
disagreeing about how to pound nails
arguing vehemently over how to make good coffee
Marcus Aurelius   Spartacus   Plato and François Villon
And it used to frustrate him terribly
that even when I was wrong he couldn't prove it
and when I agreed with him he was always suspicious
and thought he must be wrong because I said he was right
Every night the house shook from his snoring
a great motor driving us on into daylight
and the vibration was terrible
Every morning I'd get up and say 'Look at the nails—
you snored them out half an inch in the night—'
He'd believe me at first and look and get mad and glare
and stare angrily out the window while I watched 10 minutes of
        irritation
drain from his eyes onto fields and farms and miles and miles of
        snow

We quarreled over how dour I was in early morning
and how cheerful he was for counterpoint
and I argued that a million years of evolution
from snarling apeman had to be traversed before noon
and the desirability of murder in a case like his
and whether the Etruscans were really Semites

the Celtic invasion of Britain   European languages   Roman law
we argued about white being white (prove it dammit) &
    cockroaches
bedbugs in Montreal   separatism   Nietzsche   Iroquois
    horsebreakers on the prairies
death of the individual and the ultimate destiny of man
and one night we quarreled over how to cook eggs
In the morning driving to town we hardly spoke
and water poured downhill all day at the lake for it was spring
when we were gone with frogs mentioning lyrically
Russian steel production figures on Roblin Lake which were almost
    nil
I left him hitch hiking on #2 Highway to Montreal
and I guess I was wrong about those eggs

In Montreal Milton went back to his room on St. Urbain St. I went to British
Columbia shortly after. When I rejoined my wife in Montreal he was in Toronto,
and later went to Vancouver. Our ways have separated, tho not completely.
We meet every now and then, accidentally or intentionally, and remain friends.

✦2

These hewn poems have the queer bite and abrasiveness of reality. Among the
mass of public relations poetry breaking out in North America today—verse
with little use except as down-payment on a Guggenheim—they stand out with
an odd antediluvian air. They're like artifacts of a nobler, more durable age.
    In appearance, Milton Acorn himself is vividly antediluvian: heavy brow
ridges, a face carved out of red rock, and a build that suggests the cave
rather than the drawing-room. I can't imagine anyone less like a PR man,
a TV producer or any other kind of slickie. I remember seeing him once,
standing half way up a cliff in pouring Laurentian rain. It was a startling
apparition—like the materialization of some local rock-god.

From a review by Bryan McCarthy in "The Canadian Forum"

    That's a pretty good picture of Milton Acorn, and it isn't really much
exaggerated. But the most important fact about him—and this he would tell
you without being asked—is that he is a Marxist poet, a Communist. (In fact
he's the only Communist poet in Canada. Others, such as Joe Wallace, have
been mere jingling versifiers by comparison.)
    But it is a paradox that Acorn has quarreled violently with every socialist
organization he ever had anything to do with, and is a member in good standing
of none. In short, Milton Acorn is a red-necked maverick, both in politics and
poetry.
    In Montreal about ten years ago Acorn and I visited Leonard Cohen in the
atter's apartment. If ever two men were the antithesis of each other it's

Cohen and Acorn. The first elegant, even in morning disarray, self-possessed and entirely aware, moving within a slight but perceptible aura of decadence—decadence not in the sense of decline, but of standing aside and apart, not being intimately involved. And Acorn: a red fire hydrant wearing blue denims, genuine haltingly articulate, recently emerged from the noble servitude of labor, completely out of his element in that distinguished apartment which bore all the marks of Leonard Cohen's own personality.

After coffee (the thick stuff they brew in Paris—I forget its name) the conversation got around to politics. (It always does if Acorn is involved.) Cohen said, "Milton, if Communism is ever outlawed in Canada, and the Mounties round up all subversives, you'd be among the first arrested." I don't remember what Milt said to that, but I think he denied it. Of course it's true: Acorn stands out from whatever background like a neon sign on the dark side of the moon. He doesn't sneak around corners distributing leaflets, he'd be more likely to walk into Jean Drapeau's office and present him with a copy of the Collected Works of V.I. Lenin. Or send a singing telegram of the Internationale to John D.'s grandson, Nelson.

Of course Milton would be arrested immediately in a round-up of Communists. But they'd let him go the same day after a brief interrogation. The Mounties wouldn't take him seriously (perhaps only someone like Lubor Zink could), and they'd be wrong, as Cohen was wrong in his assessment, not in the fact of arrest but in not taking him seriously.

Milton Acorn is a dedicated Communist, in the same way that some of the best Christians are not formal members of the church. But with him Communism is more idealism than Marxist philosophy.

He probably knows the Manifesto by heart, but I doubt that he would label the Russian invasion of Czechoslovakia (going on as I write this) as anything other than a crime against humanity. (As is the Vietnam war, for that matter.)

What I want to convey about Acorn is paradox. If simplistic labels were feasible then Cohen would be a decadent PR man of genius, an aging Ronald Firbank tuned-in to the young on a middle-aged wavelength. Acorn would be more of a passionate and tender-hearted anarchist than Communist (and I would be a cynical Canadian nationalist, a lyrical Farley Mowat maybe).

I'd better talk about the poems. Here's what George Bowering says about "Jawbreakers":

Milton Acorn has a persistence to let nothing rest, to abide no defense or acceptance of the social status quo. It is at the elemental social level that I would like to describe him as a political poet. Further I would say that it is only at this level that poetry should have anything to do with politics, because as with so many other things, language can be emasculated at the so-called higher level of political philosophy or political "science."

So Acorn is topical, somewhat romantic in the best sense, and public. In his voice he is confident, even-paced and active. Nothing is more noticeable in his poetry than its directness and an unfaltering certainty of opinion.

That "elemental social level" Bowering mentions irritates me. Aren't all the best political poems elemental? Isn't Pablo Neruda elemental, passionate and romantic? Bad poems depend on the poet for badness, not on the subject of the poems.

Acorn's poems for me are marked by idealism and compassion for people. In some of them it's possible to discern the shadowy figures of, say, Bertolt Brecht and Mayakovsky; but I don't think there's any influence from other poets except in the matter of techniques. I think only Brecht and Mayakovsky have any direct bearing on Acorn. (Tho I know he would add the unlikely figure of Hugh McDiarmid.)

But politics is only one side of Milton Acorn. He also writes lyrics of nature, sensitive love poems, pieces that see inside the human character like a cardiogram of the intellect. As well, some beautiful evocations of his native Prince Edward Island.

> Since I'm Island-born home's as precise
> as if a mumbly old carpenter,
> shoulder-straps crossed wrong,
> laid it out,
> refigured to the last three-eighths of a shingle.

For those who may not know, carpenters once used the taper of shingles for everything from wedges to exact measurement of intangibles. "Mumbly old carpenters" probably still use them in some localities. There's a warm and human touch in such poems, especially in "Sky's Poem for Christmas."

> Christmas I became that ho-ho-ho of a saint
> to wind on a piebald disbelieving burro
> along the wisemen's trail thru a desert of grown-up people—

At his best Acorn has a feeling for humanity, in general and particular—their laughter and their tragedies—that I think is the high point of his work. In "Callum" he talks about a novice miner killed in a pit accident that may not have been quite an accident. After the boy was killed Acorn says:

> Look anywhere:
> at buildings bumping on clouds,
> at spider-grill bridges:
> you'll see no plaque or stone for men killed there:
>   but on the late shift
> the drill I'm bucking bangs his name in code—

Poems written from 1964 to 1968 have changed in style and somewhat in content from the earlier poems. The subject matter is sometimes more "public." Acorn is now more liable than ever to write about people such as Che Guevara, General Ridgway and Mohammed Ali, rather than, say, Red, the waitress. In a way I regret these stylistic and thematic differences; but all poets build on the past, and it would be against the laws of nature if acorns didn't change into oaks.

The stylistic changes particularly are very marked. Acorn has become in many poems—and I hesitate to use the word—more "diffuse," During the years prior to 1964 his poems were hard, muscular, chiseled out of verbal rock and very much to the point. Now some of them—not all—read as if the writer had infinite time to describe every detail and mused on all of them lovingly. I would instance "Tears the Dew of Beauty's Mourning." This is a difficult poem to read, because you wonder if there's any single point to be made, any real conclusion to be reached. It wanders from one concept to another with scarcely any sequence, or so it seems. And yet this poem, dated 1967, is a penetrating soliloquy on death, pain and evil. That's all I want to say without robbing the poem, for it says everything and makes me reluctant to describe it further.

I mention "Tears" as an example of Acorn's "diffuseness," generally taken to be an unflattering word, but not in his case. "Poem Written in a One-Tree Forest" is another of this genre. Somehow these poems do give the impression of infinite time, the fading detail on the underside of a leaf, verisimilitude to life—no longer punched out of rock: such a tracery of tangential thoughts that one very nearly experiences small cardiac and cerebral shocks while the poem unfolds, unpretentiously and certainly unpredictably.

It's a style that accommodates the leisure soliloquy, thought probing slowly for an opening, which relegates impatience to a corner of the mind, and may find its point in a small phrase or subordinate clause in the middle of the poem rather than a brassy clang of cymbals at the end. After we have become accustomed to Acorn's early style we do not quite know what to make of the later one. And yet, I've come to believe, the last two poems I've mentioned, as well as certain others, have an effect on the mentality comparable to flickering northern lights spreading across half a continent, much too large an area for the very familiar regional thunderstorms in the nerves and cortex.

Most litcrits would say the two short stories included in this book are "poet's short stories," by which is meant dreamy and otherworldly, as of course these two are. In most cases where the term is used it is meant to be both flattering and denigrating at the same time. It certainly shoves them into much too easy a category, for the stories are not ones that could be written by any other poet in Canada. They are a complete surprise, especially coming from a word-buster like Acorn.

It's possible to analyze them, of course, to say that "The Legend of the Winged Dingus" is a parable against war, and asserts with tongue-in-cheek that the natural human instincts and functions are beautiful and should not be artificially restrained. "The Red and Green Pony" implies that a free world of the imagination is possible if we'd only stop nattering at each other; and the story also has a definite psychological basis (did he get it out of my four-vol. Freud set?).

However, I'd rather call both stories simple magic, for each is a long-term spell cast on the reader. I'm a pretty factual person myself, and yet no matter how many times I read these stories or type them—they get to me. And I start to wonder: could there be a world like that? Well, if there can't be, the next best thing is Acorn's stories. My belief amounts to a naive certainty that both are masterpieces.

George Bowering speaks of directness in Acorn's poems. It's certainly there, especially in the early work. He doesn't mince words for anyone's digestion, tho never uses invective for its own sake, i.e. for shock value. In fact, if one reads Acorn's work carefully it will be found that he is a highly moral poet. I don't mean that in just the political sense, and certainly not that he stands for magisterial law and order, good housekeeping and conventional marriage.

Acorn speaks from a personal conception of utopian order, as full citizen of a world that never was and perhaps never will be. All his poems are written from this viewpoint, poems of absolutes, black and white poems: evil is evil and good is good, and never shall the painter's palette or the politician's double tongue turn either to a wishy-washy grey. It's a stance that sometimes appears naive, occasionally mistaken; but never insincere, always with a voice of power and conviction.

Acorn believes in the perfectability of people, the infinite capacities and hidden potentials within the individual man—these qualities being inherent and standard equipment with the ordinary person; but not there at all in those who are politically or commercially corrupted.

As I said, it's a black and white universe that Acorn inhabits. Most of the time—in fact nearly always—these absolutes lend a power to his work that is foreign to contemporary poets. Acorn himself would say that these other poets don't care enough to take stands, try to change the world, rare up on their hind legs and speak their minds in loud, vulgar and must-be-heard noises.

Milton Wilson has commented that these qualities in Acorn make him appear to be an exotic among the current voices in poetry (so much the worse for the current voices in poetry). Well, an "exotic" is something brought in from outside, imported from foreign parts, and that Acorn is not. I suppose Marxism is imported in the strictest sense, but idealism and the "brotherhood of man" have been with us for a long time, may even spread to the U.S. State Dept. or the Kremlin someday.

The truth is that most litcrits think like George Bowering: they don't really want poets to express political opinions or write nasty polemics about injustice that name names and label phonies: but to do Bowering justice, I believe he has since changed his mind about this. The guild of poets is also against it. Well, Acorn doesn't belong to the guild of poets, or any other guild, including the Communist one. They wouldn't tolerate him, and he couldn't tolerate them.

The Acorn-picture I want to convey is of a maverick and outsider, a man who speaks out at the wrong time, asks embarrassing questions of human society, and will not be satisfied by evasions. The fact that the man who asks the questions is humanly fallible and often angrily impulsive makes some kind of answers to his questions no less urgent.

It's a melodramatic portrait of Acorn, perhaps: a man replete with contradiction and paradox: but I think gives an impression of the man that is essentially accurate. A man who, in a handful of poems, comes somewhere close to greatness. Ideally he lives in the child's dream country of the two short stories in this book, and wakes up every morning in the real world that inspires him with such savage discontent.

AL PURDY

NOTE

This book consists of: two poems from "In Love and Anger," 1956; all the poems from "The Brain's the Target," 1960; several poems from the broadsheet, "Against a League of Liars," 1961; most of "Jawbreakers," 1963. Also included are many poems from the Acorn issue of "The Fiddlehead," edited by Fred Cogswell, Spring, 1963. In addition there are many new poems, written since 1963, and never collected in book form. Two short stories are also included. Poems of 1964 and later follow the two stories in the book.

It might be noted that several of Acorn's poems mention Purdy. Despite the extreme danger of the reader thinking this is a mutual admiration society of egotists, I believe these are good poems and include them. At one time Acorn and myself were about as close to blood brothers as you can get outside an Indian village. We exchanged ideas, techniques and shirts, arguing ferociously. And while it's a certainty that we influenced each other, it may be a good thing that "there needs to be no losers."

AWP

Left to right: poets Irving Layton, Milton Acorn and Eli Mandel (Montreal Star Photo courtesy Metropolitan Toronto Library Board)

Milton Acorn with Al Purdy (Montreal Star Photo courtesy the Metropolitan Toronto Library Board)

CONTENTS

I'VE TASTED MY BLOOD

If this brain's over-tempered
consider that the fire was want
and the hammers were fists.
I've tasted my blood too much
to love what I was born to.

But my mother's look
was a field of brown oats, soft-bearded;
her voice rain and air rich with lilacs:
and I loved her too much to like
how she dragged her days like a sled over gravel.

Playmates? I remember where their skulls roll!
One died hungry, gnawing grey perch-planks; *
one fell, and landed so hard he splashed;
and many and many
come up atom by atom
in the worm-casts of Europe.

My deep prayer a curse.
My deep prayer the promise that this won't be.
My deep prayer my cunning,
my love, my anger,
and often even my forgiveness
that this won't be and be.
I've tasted my blood too much
to abide what I was born to.

---

*One of the greatest misprints of all time. The intended word was
'porch-planks'.

PASTORAL

That sudden time I heard
the pulse of song in a thrush throat
my windy visions fluttered
like snow-clouds buffeting the moon.

I was born into an ambush
of preachers, propagandists, grafters,
("Fear life and death!" "Hate and pay me!")
and tho I learned to despise them all
my dreams were of rubbish and destruction.

But that song, and the drop-notes
of a brook truckling thru log-breaks and cedars,
I came to on numb clumsy limbs,
to find outside the beauty inside me.

POEM IN JUNE

A breeze wipes creases off my forehead
and my trees lean into summer,
putting on for dresses,
day-weave,
ray-weave, sap's green nakedness.

Hushtime of the singers;
wing-time, worm-time
for the squab with its crooked neck and purse-wide beak.
(On wave-blown alfalfa, a hawk-shadow's coasting.)

As a sail fills and bounds with its business of wind,
my trees lean into summer.

PARTING

My love's got secrets
of dreamplace, sounds
in her ear's core,
keys my fingers
have never played.

Deeds are folded
inside her, some of them
maybe with me.

She's sorting out
our library,
her book, my book,
and now and again
we exchange a touch
for old times.

I SPUN YOU OUT

I spun you out
Of my eyes' fire;
It wasn't you
But my desire

For the pure vein
Of silver
Running there
Even if not mine;

But I have it now,
Out of my wish
I created it
And can slough

3

Off the idiocies
I constructed of you,
Can look through
My hopeful lies

To your sorry
Hopes of yourself,
And your mysterious
Flawed glory.

POEM

          Desire
         that's in
           me,

       be souvenir
        of my last

           (O
         not lost
      where the palms
        of memory
          touch)

          love,

      and my promise
         — or
     even if not a promise,

         still be
        the reality
         of her,
        of woman.

POEM FOR THE ASTRONAUTS

As a wild duck painted sunrise colors
blurs his wings with speed
to a land known only to his heart's thrill
so man's truest home is the wind
created of his breath
and he breathes deepest in mystery.

New stars. Figures in the heavens.
Voices. How full
must be the vessel, the eye
that searches emptiness!

Canada is the scent of pines.
I left my land and returned
to know this and become Canadian.
To be an earthman I must leave Earth:
And what is Earth?
The whisper of grass?

Seeds turbulent
with fearful exultance
voyaging . . .

An Indian running the desert
kept a stone under his tongue
to drink the saliva, and
his skin remembered a thousand light touches
— fingers of his beloved.

DEATH POEM

Viki's crying
over a kitten
dead
and the waters
of my brain shake.

God, what is this whisper
of Your existence?

Today the radio blared
news of Marilyn's death.
She, bold with joy
never allowing grief,
left us holding the bag
. . . a suicide.

I never had to believe
in God, He
believed in me
I've been sure.
Did He believe in Marilyn
and the kitten I buried?

Dead, the atoms lose
intricate jointure,
muscles clot and a
skull once washed with visions
is silent,
milk-stained lips
stiffen.

Viki's tears etch
my insides,
search me
for empty places,
unstick the walls
and open them.
I fear and question
the man I'm becoming.

THE ONE-EYED SEAMAN

One violet eye open in a glass stare,
he'd dozed all night in a metal chair,
reminded me so much of you and your old strength
that I bought him coffee for breakfast.

He chuckled around his warmed belly,
this skeptic believing in a strong pulse,
so fierce in his likes, joyous in his hates
he reminded me of you, who
haven't gone hungry for a long time
and find despair a comfort.

THAT LOOK

That look
suddenly naked
the old maid
gave me

(me seeing
myself in it
as I wished to be seen

. . . curly,
muscular,
squatted there,
eyes mocking
their own gentleness)

what could I,
not loving her,
so fumbling
at any imitation
do about it?

GIRL

Inward I'm the image
of you . . . Your eyes
are a green age
I sometimes live, wise

that you're an electric
song of atoms in me,
a laugh, a trick
of sense when we touch;

but more, more, the rest
is wonder. Girl, girl,
a mockery out of the quest-
ing centre of you
feeds me — I grow pearls

like an oyster
around the flash
behind an eyelash,
an enigmatic word.

HOUSE

Building forms in a mudhole
under the old man's eye,
I said, "Look up!"
at three geese skooting low.

I loved that fusty old
muttering man,
always looking, up, down,
    to the left or
    right of you.

        (He'd scan earth
        at his feet
        as if the house
        stood there,
        him figuring,
        edging,
        adjusting.)
I loved him.

So I bugged him. Told him:
"Listen to the song sparrows,
they've divvied up this property.
We're their people."
or "My balls ring
in tune with this hammer."
I wanted to see his nose
perk and take a good sniff
of the spring air;
        but knew
        sooner or later
        he'd fire me.

THE RETIRED CARPENTER

Tools, grips sweat-polished,
in a dinted box, loose
at all angles,
half of them vanished.

No gripes today if
old Stan stops too often
to fire up his pipe.

9

SAINT-HENRI SPRING

Spring I remember wild canaries,
gusts of dandelions
and green tongues of trees
in thoughts of shy ones.

Spring I see a rubber in the gutter,
a broom-handle on a mud lawn;
thaw-water trickles from a pyin*udder.

I only see black petals
in the eyes of girls
self-contained as nettles,
choke-cherry sweet in hours
when even the slum grows flowers.

Spring I'm dwelt by startles of canaries,
coronal nudity
stuck to by drab threads of January.

*In recitation, the word I say is 'pusey'—full of pus. But it was so often mistaken for 'pussey'—a kitten—I resorted to printing it as 'pyin'—meaning of course—'full of pus'.

ENCOUNTER

Called from marking
his measured, studied
and guessed sawcut,
the carpenter

rubs back his rusty
forelock, his eyes
groping wide from shiny
cheek-sweat as if

shaken out of a dream
while he tries to fit
his thin (always thin
to him) knowledge

into the bewilderment
of a half-described
blueprint; while
gaining presence

he lets each word,
slant of your chin,
each eyelid flicker
drip from level to level

in his brain
and be counted . . .
trying to fit you too
into his pictures.

NOVEMBER

The blue-jays squeal: "More rain! More rain!"
The sky's all blotch and stain.
The colors of Earth are melted down
To dark spruce green and dull grass brown.

Black ducks, last week, held parliament
Up-river there . . . Gulls came and went.
Now that they're gone, nor'wester blown,
The grim gulls wheel and bob alone.

Nary a leaf has kept its hold.
The thicket's naked, black and cold.
Then zig-zag, like a skating clown,
The first white flake comes down.

BLACKFISH POEM

Sunglare and sea pale as tears.
One long hour we watched the black whales
circling like dancers,
sliding dark backs out of water,
waving their heaved tails,
about an eyepupil-round spot
just a knife-edge
this side of the horizon.*

*Later this became half of WHALE POEM. Before whaling became
illegal in the Gulf it was taboo on the Island to report a sighting of
great whales. Sure they were a pest, but a loose mouth might bring in a
greater pest—whalers. The beasts were in fact great whales.

OFFSHORE BREEZE

The wind, heavy from the land, irons the surf
to a slosh on silver-damp sand.
The sea's grey and crocheted with ripples;
but shadows, the backs of waves,
lengthen and lapse in the dim haze,
hinting of farther, rougher doings.

The boats went out early, but now
come worm-slow thru haze and distance.
Their gunnels invisible, the men and engines
dots moving on a spit of foam,
they travel past my vision, past
that red jag of a headland, to harbor.

LEE SIDE IN A GALE

Black sea and shone-thru sky
all mixed up along
a jumpity-jagged, beat-up
mercury saw of a skyline.

That rusty old cape hides me
but wind pokes round for me,
worries me like a scarecrow, howls
like a train from no-direction
then all-of-a-sudden whacks me.

THE SCHOONER

Keen the tools, keen the eyes,
white the thought of the schooner
lined on a draughting board,
fine the stone that ground the fine blade
and skills, the many fingers
that stroked and touched it surely
till, intricate delicate strong
it leans poised in the wind:

The wind that has its own ways,
pushing eddying rippling invisible
in light or darkness;
now no engineer or engine
can guide you but
only the delicacy of touch against touch
underneath the breathing heaven.

13

I'D LIKE TO MARK MYSELF

I'd like to mark myself
quiet, like one serene
calligraph in a color
so subtle it should only
be imagined (something

like a tree in winter
bear its lines and clusters
of snow, as if what's fallen
on it were its own).

I'd like to be quiet
except for a queer grin
that tells nothing but
whatever your own want
takes it as meaning.

But if I'm ever like that
don't believe me. You'll
know that I'm kind of
like a bud . . . that I'm

waiting for the moment
when I can project
the tip of my tongue
and taste a raindrop

warm.

THE GOLDENRODS ARE COMING UP

The goldenrods are coming up
Late in the year, in all neglected places;
Our neglect is care for them.

They are pushing through the wild grasses,
the wild grasses turning to grain.
Outside my doorstep there are three withered heads
Of wild alfalfa tangled with goldenrod —

Like three princes of an old family
Trying to hold their land
While their heads turn dull;
The goldenrod twists them with
Its every nod, working at
Their roots and stems
like a rising moneylender.

AN UNTIDY ROOM

*An untidy room
is my heart
, because I
can't bear to sweep out
all
of any man*

*; and the parts left in
are attached by cordy
things that straggle
over the threshold, so I
can't shut the door
tight.*

15

MONUMENT

With gentleness
his eyes filmed
in his smile,
and he said

"The gaschamber boys
got my whole family;
I married
to give the vision
which is life
again to the line."

His son, with none
of life's handwriting
yet on his face,
played, and around him
the ghosts stood gossiping.

SUMMER: DOWNTOWN MONTREAL

In the heat, beggars multiply,
clothes smokey-grey as the air,
faces the color of the pavement
the legless ones sprawl on;
each with a cap flopped beside him,
its clutch of silver and pennies.

Each one has his stand.
 No one encroaches.
I wonder who brings them here,
who picks them up,
and who they share the take with.

THE LOST LEADER

(To Irving Layton)

I remember me, young prol
in a short haircut, ignorant
and proud of it,
going to his house

where he read my arrogant rhymes
, not critical, joyous
as if to share
my florid romance:

and what words I had for him
were grudging. If

I could go back now
and kiss him on both cheeks!
but I had my own concepts
; knew nothing
of the winds that cut
lonely rocks:

and I suppose imagined
each of us
always
strong.

ROOMING HOUSE

Somebody's retching
down the hall, it
goes on for hours
every day.

Fine background music
for a poem! And then
there's the singing
of the old man
scavenging the garbage;

who used to teach history
so he says. I guess
he was something
besides what he is.

Funny, how time
strips us down
to what maybe
we really are. *

One I met in the corridor
had no shoes, only rubbers
flapping on his feet.

As for me I've got no clock
and when I moved in
figured all the alarms
would wake me.

Next morning I overslept.
Everybody here
is on social assistance.

*This verse—one of my most commented on—is horseshit. The Black
Mountain Gang was 'rising' (if it can be called that) and my attitude
was: "You guys think you can write horseshit? Here's real horseshit!"

WHY A CARPENTER WEARS HIS WATCH
INSIDE THE WRIST

They say it's guarded better
there, from the bumps of the trade.

I disproved this, and

guessed first those patched people
stuck up like chimneys
in high places, fix them
there so's to look at them
with no long upsetting armswing,
just a turn of the wrist,

but the gruesome truth is
that with the gargoyle-pussed
boss watching, they
don't worry much about balance;

which led me to the real reason
they wear watches tucked close
bouncing and scratching
among all their tools . . .

it's so they can look quick
out of the lefteyecorner
without the foreman seeing.

BOY FISHING AT A PIER

Wisps of breeze
curl one way
then another
in air soaked yellow
with sunlight.

His hot skin
licks the wind;
thoughts, images
of the rotting harbor
slew slow *
under a thatch
of hair hot to touch.

His legs dangle down,
small waves fritter at
the green-hung pile
crusted in spots
with barnacle villages.

His line wavers down
to the ripples, and
down into the drink-
ing swirl, fleck-
ering life, light.

Sharp thoughts of fishes.
A color stabs one
and his guts thrill.

Sharp thoughts of fishes.
Leave the stupid conformist
his edifying dream
of others even stupider than himself.

Sharp thoughts of fishes,
all life is light
earth and water,
but first light
then short darkness,

*Originally 'stew slow'—a printer's improvement, gladly accepted.

but spiralling up
atoms trickling
to light again
even thru saw-rip-
ping teeth staining
water briefly red,

to feed the sun
in the eye that
the sun in the sky
ignites to fill
the brain with light.

Taut, relaxed,
taut relaxed under
stretching gold
skin a muscle lives
as life chases, tears,
luring with colors, spins
smaller and smaller, dying
in the moment of delight.

A scaled body works,
the tail works,
the gills work
flooded with tastes of
the harbor drinking the sea,
nibbling the land,
tongue touching the cool
droplets of a splash.

A sweat-drop glistens,
rolls, catches
on a glittering hair.

Spine curved erect, his singing
skull's fluid balance, his
penis a wee rosebud,
its thrill withdrawn
softly, singingly
into his entrails,
light's joy travelling
miles of capillaries.

JOE DYING

When Joe said, "I'm dying,"
it couldn't damp me,
in his presence
one chuckles for joy.

His truths so innocent,
his lies so innocent,
Joe's innocent,
I'm innocent,
death's innocent.

For the dead
there is no death,
one way or another
not even nothing.

But Joe and those
hearts beating outside mine.
Each one lost crumbles off me,
a piece I've got to regrow.

MORE INTRICATE

More intricate
than ferns,
the keys of being.

Before this writing
you stood opaque.

My poem and
now this
suddenness of seeing.

POEM POEM

Yesterday a bust of breath
Poems* broke from the white dam of my teeth.
I sang truth, the word I was;
And with each shout curling my tongue
Heart and fist thumped together.

But the poem I write today grins
While I chop it like a mean boy,
And whittles my spine.
Insinuating friend or stranger
It is truth, the word I am not.

*"Poem"—The word is singular.

A WORRIED BUT EASY HABIT

The past (for that's the only past
there is) is wound up inside me,
Old Man, that's our trouble.
The past when you used to gargle
your rage in the morning;
and I was an enemy, quick
with the desperate curse of truth.

But that's my trouble, Old Man;
a worried but easy habit
of "Enemy in sight: Open Fire!"
And with you changed, your face
with a smile washed onto it,
I go on jabbing, provoking,
fighting a ghost in a bad cloud.
That's our trouble, Old Man.
Forgive, me, for today
and tomorrow start with forgiveness.

23

AUTUMN, AN ERA

An amnesiac wakened in autumn
by the scurrying furred fingers of the squirrels
mistook its flux for motion.

He saw land voiced and beating as an ocean,
the unquiet gianthood of clouds, *
as their flight went turning on its tendrils.
In leafy wind-whorls, yellow and red, he thought it
a good time to wake in, time to hum loud
like a sage in turbulent bright Ilium
approached by Achilles' black-prowed squadron.

Nothing allowed him a chill guess
of winter when life waits in dens
and frost fastens its intense stillness.

*There's a line dropped here. Damned if I can reconstruct it.

THE PLUNGE

Underneath muscles bloodrich and woven
my bones shake
to suddenly know myself beloved
by you, strong and all of a woman.

That word love only tickles
my lip between giggles
until you sing
my name calling me to stand tall
. . . and that's a swaying thing.

I feel a jolly decorated male bee
about to explode in love's shudder,
like going up in a highspeed elevator
with no floor — only handholds.

But let down your hair, love; let it down
so it hangs low as my navel;
and I'll hold on love, hold on
till we hop all tangled in joy
the whole length of Hell.

REBUTTALS

1

Dear fine-eyebrowed poet
writing of "vengeful owls";
before we use up truth
our tongues'll slough off.
Why waste time telling lies?

2

You with measuring eyes under
lids rumpled like bedclothes;
I know you dote on categories
but why jam me in one?
We've talked just seven seconds.

3

You've slung your truisms like
cases clanking with beer-bottles,
played amateur propagandist and
bayoneted a line of dummies.
Now what do you really think?

4

So . . . You've damned fools and
reduced time and its stars turning
themselves and space into light
to the compass of an argument?
I don't think everything should stop.

OF MARTYRS

I often think of martyrs
and when I do the wind shakes,
and with that pity I can touch their lives,
their flesh,
for they were the most loving of folk.

It was life they chose
not death,
not the staccato small deaths
that leave life a ghost of memories
not really remembered.

They wouldn't lop one verse
from the song of their lives,
wouldn't say the dull fantastic prose
the crazy chants of liars.

Til the last stride with a living instep,
they chose life, not death.*

*I had Ethel and Julius Rosenberg in mind.

THE HANDS

Why man, those hands, dyed
earth and tobacco brown, tough
as an old alligator suitcase, fissured
a dozen extra ways, have
a grip all courtesy, a touch
delicate and sure as a young woman's.

26

MY LOVE, A FIERCE ALTRUIST...

My love, a fierce altruist,
Walks on a path which few would dare;
Over a perilous black abyss,
A slender tight-rope in the air.

And sometimes, with no side-long glance,
But glum and introspective stare,
She walks as if she owned it all
Straight out upon the misty air.

IN MEMORY OF TOMMY, AN ORPHAN, WHO WAS KIDNAPPED FROM HIS LOVING FOSTER-MOTHER, KATHERINE, IN FULFILLMENT OF A BARGAIN BETWEEN CHURCHES

No wonder the boy dreamt of monsters
terrible in horns, mooing his name,
chasing to tickle and eat him; no wonder
these drownpools of eyes looked in
the second storey window, their bland face
brooding cruel grown-up abstractions;
no wonder that dinosaur with the cooing
dove voice, too big to hide in a barn:
no wonder he woke with terror caught
like a fishbone in his throat, to huddle
amidst a dark full of faces.

I don't know if hate's the armer of love;
what side he joined, or if he joined: but
when he learned to hate those dreams ended.

THE TOLERANT PHILISTINE

If behind that toothpaste grin,
one eyeball one way, one the other,
sets an adding-machine going tick-bang, click-clang;
if he'd amputate his mother's wedding-ring finger
for the price of a girly show:

tolerate it, brother,
tolerate it.
Realize he's human.

And this man makes his wife
a dunghill to crow on;
his "damn's," "you did's," and "you didn'ts,"
a fist-full of small flies
eternally at her eyelids:
tolerate it, brother,
tolerate it.
Realize he's human.

If it's all strictly for vultures,
a few smart operators, mere cheerful idiots,
and the rest living in a flaccid paroxysm;
its morals and LIFE editorials *
a recitation for laughing hyenas:

tolerate it, brother,
tolerate it.
Realize they're human.

But if a poet grows a beard
and calls you a truthful name; if some pickets
hopped up on coffee and empty stomachs
squash a scab; if men's feet, pierced
and fixed with horseshoes,
kick:

never tolerate that!
Why, such tolerance could upset
your whole system of tolerance!

*LIFE—a savage American propaganda magazine—now defunct.

28

ONCE I LAY ON A MATTRESS

Once I lay on a mattress
smoking a cigar, smoking thoughts
tonguing my skull.

Ruthless with happiness
black as a burn, I
saw human needs, each absolute,
moving against each other;

as my thoughts rose against each other,
each destroying the last.

Agonies of bodies and brains
caught in the vise of change
or hunger, or the money game,
stubborn wrongs of upright minds,
fed the smoking rose of my content.

Workings, workings of the dialectic,
forces, forces, I told myself
and curled like smoke from my cigar,
but the walls creaked in the frost
and somewhere a poor whore shivered.

HAIKU

I light my cigar
on a tree's lee side
while a dog waits politely.

POEM

My mother goes in slippers
and her weight thumps the floor,
but when I think of her I think of one smile
when she was young

and to me was a goddess of green age
tho now I remember her young
with hair red as a blossom.

I remember the whole room full of that smile
and myself scampering across the edges.

Now she lives on cigarettes and wine,
goes from potted plant to flower,
knowing the time and manner
of each one's tending.

ROBERT

(*For R. Rousil*)

We haven't written letters
not needing to remind ourselves
that he's himself there
and I'm myself here.

Once we went over each other
like with rough hands, arguing
for every hard corner of a reason
stuck out on each of us.

But that each was each we agreed
and because we were two . . . one.

We actually met once, since;
he wrinkled up a grin, I nodded
we said hello.

We haven't written letters
not needing to remind ourselves
that the things we do make roots
sucking sweet water.

Like he's a tree out there
I can stretch out to lean on.
He won't move.

THE MACHINE-GUNNER

They wanted to quit
but I'd been taught;
wits and trigger
caught in a knot.

A squeeze as light as nothing
. . . so.
They drilled and drilled
So's I'd know,

when noise jangled
my brain's two halves
and piss spiralled
down my calves

and pressing a wave
chugged a black barge
my sight crawled on
a bed-bug enlarged

and the shirt white as chalk
yanked up and down thru flutters
my tracers snatched.
Thru shock,

some one was yelling
"They want to quit!"
Behind my creased forehead
I thought of it:

but sights held on
and gun belled on
till the belt was gone
and screaming done.

If I sleep tonight
that black barge will float
overhead on the dirty water
choking my throat. *

*Like most of my narrative poems, this incident is actual. The
gunner was not me.

RESTAURANT SCENE

Take Red the waitress
scrawny and guts and things
sticking every which way,
yet along with her bones she hitches
a corona, a halo of herself.

Take her customer, bitch lady-type,
brains compressed to lips' thinness,
yet in Red's aura her talcumed face
relaxes into humanity: her voice
rejoices not far from a chuckle.
Now Red's gone and that mouth's
prepared for cruel words, clamped
by cruel ropes of muscle.

IN ADDITION

In addition to the fact I lost my job for a nosebleed

In addition to the fact my unemployment insurance stamps were just
     one week short

In addition to the fact I'm standing in line at the Sally Ann for a
     breakfast of one thin baloney sandwich and coffee

In addition to all that it's lousy coffee.

THE DAMNATION MACHINE

Hell's the place
of the disarmed innocents
who can't use the purge of rage.

It's long since they've been penetrated
by sorrow; their souls are
a smudged page
where nothing can be written.

All wars have been fought
and lost,
won,
or just gone by,
and the weapons of the mind
hang in a void.

(Meaningless chopped prose
without the rhythm of combat,
the painting done in blood
and blackness,
the sting of joy.)

Side by side the damned walk
heel and toe in old tracks.
Their words have no bearing
on questions they've almost forgotten.

INLAND GULL

Over drab-shingled peak,
skating on land-buffed air,
white as sun-fierce snow
on a great height,
white
beneath a dirty woolen sky.

His beak, a hooked pencil-mark,
scratches arrogance on brittle gusts.
A refugee from the storm,
it seems his own:
his baleful prophecy.

HEAR WITH THE WIND STILL

Hear with the wind still, the grass still,
sharp and erect like animal ears,
its green darkened,
the air and its light dark green,

birds hidden in the just trembling
leaves, chirping hoarse wonder,
and one white butterfly dancing into shade
the rustle of the rain coming on.

LIBERTAD

LIBERTAD, the sculptor, teaches poetry
to me:
  "Freedom, my freedom
composed of the stone's, the steel's
freedom to find by me its form in
this time, this I and it, this place."

For me it's the tight-grinned nod of
a girl fighting passion as
I recite Spender; and
night and city lights' subdued
shadow of green on clouds and
nighthawks crying, bounding from
curve to taut curve in air; and
throbbing among turbines the
gutted consonantal speech of
a rigger, ex-seaman; the
ring of the struck spike bouncing
hammer and arm into the blows' beat.

And Libertad: his wire-black beard
cropped to let him mask as a welder; or
black-sweatered, all angles
strained into his deed with iron; or
talking, his tensile torso tossed
back into an arm's gesture: he too
is my poetry, my freedom. *

CHARLOTTETOWN HARBOR

An old docker with gutted cheeks,
time arrested in the used-up-knuckled hands
crossed on his lap, sits
in a spell of the glinting water.

He dreams of times in the cider sunlight
when masts stood up like stubble;
but now a gull cries, lights,
flounces its wings ornately, folds them,
and the waves slop among the weed-grown piles.

*"Libertad" is Armand Vaillancourt.

OLD PROPERTY

Past that frost-cracked rock step
twist yourself thru
skewgee trunks and old coat-hook branches;
ground once dug and thought of and
never intended for those toadstools.

In the shade past the crashed robins' nest,
past that spilt sunlight see,
his grainy grip on
a hatchet keened to a leaf,
a man in murky denims
whispering curses to the weeds.

ISLANDERS

Would you guess from their broad greeting,
witty tuck of eyelids,
how they putt-putt out with lunch-cans
on sea liable to tangle
and dim out the land between two glances?

Tho their dads toed the decks of schooners,
dodging the blustery rush of capes,
and rum-runner uncles used wit-grease
against the shoot-first Yankee cutters,
they wouldn't be the kind to sail their
        lobster-boats around the world
for anything less than a dollar-ninety an hour.

1956

BELLE

Younger, Belle was lonely, but now
the men brandish forearms in her kitchen,
shake themselves out with laughter.
The wives, glad they're not at mischief,
respect her jet black mane from a distance.

Edwin with his glasses, his pipe,
and freckled, spare-tipped fingers,
she married at twenty-nine, had to
(everyone had to, but she
claims that weakness like a certificate),
hums to himself, makes
the best cider in the settlement, hangs
doors that open to one hooked finger,
says four words in a day
and two of them are "No Ma'am!"

There's a contest of daughters
and one son,
born beside a mare munching clover.
She bore it alone, and
herself whacked it into life.

THE ISLAND

Since I'm Island-born home's as precise
as if a mumbly old carpenter,
shoulder-straps crossed wrong,
laid it out,
refigured to the last three-eighths of shingle.

Nowhere that plow-cut worms
heal themselves in red loam;
spruces squat, skirts in sand;
or the stones of a river rattle its dark
tunnel under the elms,
is there a spot not measured by hands;
no direction I couldn't walk
to the wave-lined edge of home.

In the fanged jaws of the Gulf,
a red tongue.
Indians say a musical God
took up his brush and painted it;
named it, in His own language,
"The Island."

MIKE

You, Mike, twisting on words as if
they flushed your kidneys with daylight,
your sunset's smoggy green, hot orange,
and shunters skoot throbbing thru
muddled smoke and the noises of iron.

I'm geared different, Mike, to a nod
and look over wavey water, my name
pronounced with a rolling tongue,
the sky like sails in need of washing
sometimes, then splotched blue,
the wind familiar to my shoulders.

That's me past your image of me:
and the figure I see wincing
at sirens and jack-hammer clatter
is only my image of you, and
behind it, feeding it, is you
with your grin showing one eyetooth,
reckoning the works of a man, tracing
the routes of wire or politics, exclaiming
at your own sudden understanding.

AT EL CORTIJO[*]

At *El Cortijo*, with coffee
tilting right and left
in talk weird as alcohol,
a little dark one backed
into my knee, didn't
look round . . . just sat on it.

No introduction! She took
my femur for a public perch,
and in that exhilarant
fluctuation of conversation
quivered
like a kitten ready to bounce.

I wrung myself with love
for the finely wound nerve of her,
balanced there,
and the way loose hairs
half-twisted
at her palpitating nape.

Disturbed by my rude eye
she twitched round to glare
my grin into a grimace,
then looked back
but didn't budge
her delicate handful of a bum.

*In a school text of this poem: Purdy asked. "What do you think
happened next?" Nothing...I already had a lover. The point was "la
Canadienne's" habit of using an odd body for furniture.

PROBLEM

When you look into your golden beer
and talk about suicide, Al,
I can't help dreaming laments,
obituaries, and how craftily
I'd cull my quotations
of you, half martyr
to this dusty tasting time
and half damned decadent.

Like a green lignum vitae tree,*
a nuisance on the lawn,
dead you'd carve into strong shapes,
living you're a problem.

*"The lignum vitae tree will grow in almost any pollution, hence its name "vitae"—"living". It is also lethal—poisoning the grass around its trunk.

JULY CREATURES

After the dim blue rain
swarms of innocent flying things
(green things, curly-bodied things,
things shaped like an arrowhead)
tiny with outsize wings

go wherever the wind wobbles
among pinwheeling swallows
and meet uncomprehended harm
in blond thickets on my forearm.

LYRIC

If I said love that word
'd recreate me as love,
said love you that breath
'd drop me trembly on
your breasts, your breath.

Love's before you, before me;
nearest to god we know.
Utter his name truly then he
's possessor and law.
Listen, love, I say it.

IN THE THIEF'S MINDSEYE

In the thief's mindseye our bright places
are photograph grey, and our darknesses
ways lit by his narrow intense want.

The conjurer too knows fissures in our vision
and there slips his deuces, discovers rabbits;
for it's by our needs we explore
and only become aware of shadows
when there's already a little light.

Scientists have been hoodwinked
by an old black-shawled woman, despising her
and unable to guess or believe
that a room has extra corners
a peasant can brood about and find before they.

THE TROUT POND

(For R. F. Acorn, 1897-1968)

The woods, spruce twisted
into spooky shapes,
echo the trickle of water
from raised oars.

Above the pale ripples
a redwing blackbird fastens,
legs crooked and beak alert,
to a springing reed.

My father's whiteheaded now,
but oars whose tug
used to start my tendons
pull easily these years.

His line curls, his troutfly drops
as if on its own wings,
marks a vee on the mirrored
ragged spruceheads, and
a crane flapping past clouds.

1958

THE FIGHTS

What an elusive target
the brain is! Set up
like a coconut on a flexible stem
it has 101 evasions.
A twisted nod slews a punch

a thin gillette's width
past a brain, or
a rude brush-cut to the chin
tucks one brain safe under another.
Two of these targets are
set up to be knocked down
for 25 dollars or a million.

In that TV picture in the parlor
the men, tho linked move to move
in a chancy dance,
are abstractions only.
Come to ringside, with two
experts in there! See
each step or blow pivoted,
balanced and sudden as gunfire.
See muscles wriggle, shine
in sweat like windshield rain.

In stinking dancehalls, in
the forums of small towns,
punches are cheaper but
still pieces of death.
For the brain's the target
with its hungers
and code of honor. See
in those stinking little towns,
with long counts, swindling judges,
how fury ends with the last gong.
No matter who's the cheated one
they hug like a girl and man.

It's craft and
the body rhythmic and terrible,
the game of struggle.
We need something of its nature
but not this;
for the brain's the target
and round by round it's whittled
til nothing's left of a man
but a jerky bum, humming
with a gentleness less than human.

"I WILL ARISE AND GO NOW"

Let's borrow a tent and live on The North Shore
Where the wind beats bluff from Labrador
And summer flutters by at half mast;
Cut the umbilical cord of the past
While our out-of-work benefits last.

The hungry? Let's not appease them.
If they had the power
They'd only make you paint to please them
And me punctuate my poetry.
Let's not mean, but be.

Let's sign a ban-the-bomb petition
To show we're intelligent
Then let politics go to perdition,
While you tell me and I'll tell you
How sweet we are.

I will read you Henry Miller
And you'll wear your diaphragm.
Selling out the future
And owning no geiger counter,
Let's take it on the lam.

WINTER BOARDERS

Smoke and in a blue halo let a poem grow
Of winter and sky blue as laughter
Tinting immaculate snow,
The crows fasting on their pine pulpits
And all the other birds gone, except
On a white tablecloth of snow,
The chickadees, happy and fat as a chuckle.

CYNICISM *

Notice the bums are little guys?
Caps cocked sidewise,
Too big,
Faces brown-grey and wrinkled like a fig.
Funny . . . all little guys.

Ever stand in a shape-up?
An ape of a pusher puts his finger up,
"Com'ere Joe."
And "Joe" is usually big;
Little men linger against the wall, then go.

Even to look at one's a feast
For your sense of virtue.
"Why not work," you say, " 'twont hurt you."
They get less sympathy than wingless flies.
Funny . . . all little guys.

*The able little men, once a common, edifying sight. Have been practically exterminated by the God damned bosses.

DEATH'S INCARNATION

The fool who called Death (fearing another might)
thought this creature hooded in shadows
— its face atomic light,
'ld make arrests at his crying
command only . . . but Death served itself
by serving any one — especially the dying.

Into that acrimonious assembly,
Death slid, tornado-dark
tall and making each see
his bones stripped bare in the next man's eye,
then swayed waiting like a genie
to swoop at the first cry of "Seize that villain!"
and wind them all in — a gesticulating chain.

45

Mind you, Death'd always been present,
not so obedient
but there, life's corollary
and referee,
disease's final cure, earth's sweetener
and champion of heirs . . . Fancy
a new enlightened policy
messing with the turds of dinosaurs!

"Today, with Death so eager
to obey thought or feckless gesture,
we must do without!" they chorused,
each trying to be earnest;
with so many rogues unhung, so much
devilish opinion to unravel
and rewind with Death watching
. . . so much rage unsettled.

PICASSO'S SEATED ATHLETE WITH CHILD

The child and the old man's eyes
big and wild as a stallion's.
The child I growing, wanting
towards wizardry and competence.

I've dreamt wizards so competent
suns spun side-on to
a nudge from their spare fingertips.

In his brain-pan dreams, the
intricate tension of atoms,
worlds, and him poised
about to dance into them.

46

ANNIE'S SON

Weeks after her abortion,
Clutches of bone
(A thin nearly straight one,
A rib cage, a spine)
Came into the world-light.

Last was the skull and
Pelvis . . . which she wore
For a charm.

LETTER TO MY REDHEADED SON

Young maple leaves, copper with a delicate flush,
are taut and hardly bent by the limb-twist breeze,
and I'm penetrated by the delight that made you
and makes fool poets call the spring green.

A poet against a league of liars, I know
you'll learn love and honesty from her
who wouldn't learn scorn and left me.
You'll learn, boy, to be as bitter as me
against the men with counterfeit eyes,
their graft and their words: "nigger";
"people not like us" . . . and "bastard."

Fool poets call the spring green, but I
a poet, know I can't give you to yourself
— only what I know of myself: that
nothing I've done, no poem, stand,
thought or act of love, hasn't called for
another, stronger deed, or I've lost it.

HUMMINGBIRD

One day in a lifetime
I saw one with wings
a pipesmoke blur
shaped like half a kiss
and its raspberry-stone
heart winked fast in
a thumbnail of a breast.

In that blink it
was around a briar
and out of sight, but
I caught a flash
of its brain
where flowers swing
udders of sweet cider;
and we pass as thunderclouds or,
dangers like death, earthquake, and war,
ignored because it's no use worrying.

MORE BLESSED

I need to wonder why
She did it, when
He despised her for it
As she knew he would.

Despised because he needed
To despise, but before that
Needed to be held, taken
With love given.

Now he's got both his
Love and state of despise;
And her not caring's
Part of her care, large
As the lands of the wind.

She takes blessedly
Giving with full hands.

IMAGES FOR THE SEASON

i

pussy-willows reflected
on ripples, flutter
like bands of butterflies

ii

my girl cries look
at a thin-necked robin
strained up, clearing
his throat for a song

iii

a foal among
rags of april snow
spring's wobbled up to me
and nudged me
with his milky nose.

THE TAPEWORM

Consider the hypocrite:
No denizen he of the green breathing puddle;
Before the apeman looked up
Brushing mud from his eyebrows
There was no hypocrite.

And consider the tapeworm:
No undulating swimmer in that puddle,
His eye admitting a needle of light to go by,
Would acknowledge his heir, the tapeworm.

He has a suction cup on his head,
And where delicious conduits wind
He's lapping lapping lapping
Crapping crapping crapping,
Practising sex with
No corny love christian or otherwise.

Where the strivers found the way
Comes the hypocrite with his thousand suction caps
The ideals and prayers he lives by.

His head hooked near the charging brain,
His tail goes wiggle-waggle in the sewers.
Nectar bathes the sealed caves of his eyes
But what flows past is poisonous pap.

He's rehearsed the imitation of man;
Hymns, or according the*fashion,
Curses, woofs the tones of laughter.
He's the same in every age, and
In each age thinks he's something brand new.

*"to"

ASHAYE DANCING

When Ashaye with the nerve-devouring fire
in her eyes, Ashaye
with her body's secret places,
when Ashaye dances;

The severe dark of her leotards
eats the song in the blood
while her soles slap stark and
the blacks of iron,
of hailstorms,
become her limbs and torso
forms axing, blasting
with her brain all one austere eye
brooding within its motion.

She's blots, destructions
each washing out the last
but revolving into me
so I'll go a host to them
as my thoughts'll walk one day
not as words but steel and marrow. *

My breathing's the only music
til she stills, hangs a moment
on a thought, then straightens,
loosens, becomes
Ashaye again, wild-eyed lover
mother and wilful girl.

*See: John: 1:1
In the Welsh the word ____ means *poet, worker,* or *God*. Every poet
must assume himself immortal. Whether he is or not is beside the
point. The same goes for ____.

"CALLUM"

(In memory of a novice miner)

He had hair like mustard-weed;
shoulders a scoop;
eyes a lake you see the rocks on bottom;
and his voice swung a loop
with music in what it said
that tangled inside your head.

"Callum" is*his name
— pronounced as if he'd sign it on the sun.
From "The Island" he came:
don't know which one.

We dropped to work in our cage,
hearts somewhere behind on a parachute.
That pusher was cute
— saw him a guy who'd count doing right important,
put him at a hard job beside a well
. . . a hundred and forty feet,
and he fell.

Look anywhere:
at buildings bumping on clouds,
at spider-grill bridges:
you'll see no plaque or stone for men killed there*:
    but on the late shift
the drill I'm bucking bangs his name in code
. . . "Callum":
tho where "The Island" is I'll never know.

                                        1956

* was
*Gerry Galagher has since made this untrue, in one case.

52

TWO PLAYERS

One exultant in stroke and guard,
loses himself, tastes alcohol
in the blood of his bitten lips.
The man-pack's howling
of things to be proved, fades and
he's like the driven and returned ball;
living to the limit when
one of the furies of the game.

The other, with his skin dark
as leathern gear, goes into
the game as a high ordeal,
a test like other tests
to prove his people; and
his heart, an eagle in his chest,
buffeting the cage of ribs,
mad to get out.

These two envy one another,
not for prizes but
in a way neither could imagine
unless he loved as well:
and when they battle in the pit
richocheting off the walls and each other,
you're seeing the game, man,
as it's improvised in instants
by two players juggling
calm and frenzy;
beating at the hurricane
about their hands and brains.

THE IDEA*

It's events itch the idea
into existence. The clawing
pixilating world lofts
the mind and its wrangling images
as contrary, gusty, circling
winds toss, flaunt the flags
(splendrous as if living) of
old duchies, unforgotten empires.

Then something palpable as voltage,
maybe a grim preacher, maybe
a wild thin man on a soapbox,
or even a character lugging
a pail and whitewash brush
(whitewash or smear it's all
a point of view) takes charge:
something you want in a way
savage or happy, takes charge:
the idea grows flesh, with nerves
to feel the pain of dismemberment.

But its life is death, and life's
going back to the chewing
creation obeying just itself;
so the herded clouds, dream-beasts
in the eyes' pasture, are torn
to fall like tears, like blood.
Then the idea's more like blood,
something in time with running feet,
with typewriter, with heartbeat.

*Once again I say onto you: See John: 1:1.

54

NOVEMBER BEACH

Every step in the noise
of the ocean tumbling from the skyline
to stone frozen rippled sand
is shaken in the shaking wind.

The water of your eye freezes
in one glance outward
to the ducks racing, beaks open,
tagging, zig-zagging
amidst the bullets of spray.

CANADIAN WINTER — 1960/61

Up Spadina, feet like the slow end
of a mutt sniffing from trashcan to pole,
(smutty, scruffy, sour-fat on a thin dole,
pausing whole minutes to lick his behind)
regularly — rain, tea-weak sun, or blinding
snow-glutted poundage of a cold gale —
grey, jawdroopy with ragged lips, the pale
men past forty peg to the breadline.

They've washed in the dirty water of boredom
and in thinly conscious ways are still here;
but predictable in fluctuation
as spasms of malarial fever
or winged ant exodi. My bizarre sir
stop a minute! think of the word "human."

POEM WITH FAT CATS IN THE BACKGROUND

Hungry men, their grins tight with embarrassment,
move by clever steps to intercept me
on the spit-grey downtown streets.
With my wrinkled shoes, my coat ill-used and borrowed,
I wonder how they know me.

One showed me his road-rough palms:
"Look, aren't these worker's hands?"
Oh many have tricks
to trap me — tired of rage and bored with pity,
into the pain of knowledge:
"This is real . . . This is a man!"

My worried arithmetic's blown out of my brain
and I give . . . a nickel, two dimes, a quarter.
Often they want to shake hands,
but I haven't done it yet
. . . Made a partner in Man's indignity
I ask for nothing but a curse.

SKY'S POEM FOR CHRISTMAS

As from milky vapour, dust of atoms jostling like hornets,
a nebula swigs great swatches of itself into a new sun
raw with light, ravener to its parent mists, messenger
to far astronomers thirsty for the word, the word
that'll unlock them: I've never lost a faith
or wrenched my roots of eyes from the heart . . .
Each doom to joy and torment's nourished
within an old love, becomes a new focus
pulsing radiation, disrupting
the foggy smut of death about it;

while I still step to the blood's rhythm,
the soul's reason in those old stories
of kings and white-hot new stars, wonderful babes
like Jupiter's yowl making that Island cave boom like an organ,
born to laugh a challenge at the old cruel gods.

Surely at least once when a new star burst thru heaven
three old men forsook the stern fantasies
of mummy-clothes they'd wrapped around the world,
and surely they found at least one babe
who held great bear time by its short tail . . . .
For birth by birth the many-colored creatures of Earth
break ranks and dance apart calling their names and numbers
to reassemble with shoutings and elbow-digs
in formations first seen by the mindseye of a child.

Christmas I became that ho-ho-ho of a saint
to wind on a balky piebald disbelieving burro
along the wisemen's trail thru a desert of grown-up people
like cactus with its growth stalled in tormented poses:
til housed and run around by squirrels I found the boy Sky
with eyes hazel windows into outré dimensions
now looking out on wonder, now looking in
at wonder . . . I came not with gifts but
for a present of the universe made strange, tumbling
with odd fuzzy animals, blue of high heaven
siphoned down to tank up my brain,
for meteors he caught and sent sizzling past my ears:
and for myself made quaint, totemic
like a thick oak come wobbling, walking
grotesquely on its roots over patches of dark and sunlight.

ON SAINT-URBAIN STREET *

My room's bigger than a coffin
but not so well made.
The couple on my left drink, and
at two a.m. the old man shouts
of going back to Russia.
About five he or his wrung-out wife
puke up their passage money.

The janitor (pay, five a week
plus a one-bed apartment
with furnace in kitchen) has
one laughing babe at home
and two girls, for lack of room,
in the orphanage.
On holidays they appear
with their soul-smashed faces.

Upstairs the Negro girl
answers the phone, sings my name
in a voice like a bad angel's.
Her boy-friends change
every week-end, like the movies.
But my room's cheap, tho
when the wind shifts north
I wear my overcoat
to type this bitter little poem.

*I don't stand behind this poem now.

A BASTARD'S STORY

Maybe a six-month-old
then, no more,
your eyes dim with fear,
you remember your weak self

Carried as if on the tide
of a nightmare
into that room with white coats
and meaty moons of faces.

A woman with a starched breastplate,
giant hams and shoulders,
splashed you into cold water,
slashed it into your face.

You choked, fought
a screaming tangle,
and she fought,
repressing curses; til

It seemed you saved your life,
were dried, wrapped
in a towel with a washed-out pattern,
and then you slept.

It shivers me to hear you,
an old man with beautiful hands,
saying, "I'm sure
she was trying to drown me."

"MURDER"

(on TV, and places)

Let's have no
nonsense of
the human spinning
itself into worlds
lovely with
logic
or illogic.

Logic (in
the better case)
you might have
but the man, the
breathing woman's
a grey stick in it
to snap in the
problem's workings
— odd pieces
of bloody whimsy
chuckle up the
slow passages.

Or go West young
young lad, to
learn most
sentimental lessons
illustrated
by rows of dolls
knocked over
(they never
scream or
spout blood,
don't mind
dying).

60

LIFEBLOOD SOLILOQUY

1

I see a robin on the rain-soaked lawn.
His heart's a swift electric spark
and wee legs drive in packed explosive hops.

Each action's a life-embodied thought;
each thought reflexive, instant with the deed.
Movement distilled, unseen between its poses,
his pin-holed head
listens for worms' dumb secrecy.

2

The trucks drive by towards the hill,
each with its driver's calculating ear
in the engine's multitudinous beat.

In rage, by hard-rubber teeth,
the hill's dragged down, clawed over.
Voice vaults the scale to triumph, then a gearshift
to its hallelujah of the road.

3

There's a bird whose name I've never heard *
only the variations of its song.
It comes between false dawn and dawn
to a black tree and sings to me.

I'll seep down into earth, rise and become that bird:
tune and rhythm tight in tiny brain
to spout thru tonal throat,
ring stratospheric layers with my joy.

*Unfortunately for the survival of mystery—The night song of a robin.

GIRL AT A CROSSROADS

Brain liver and whole insides
at a slow burn . . .
see the smoke in her eyes!

Like hammers rata-tata-tating
at sheet-metal, cold
rain's batting
the night road, the signpost
and she with rivulets in her hair,
hesitating, a reticule
cluttering small souvenirs
in one chill-fixed handhold.

"Go on! travel!" the whip-tongues
of rain speak . . . Rips of lightning
for hundredths of seconds
photograph place-names on the sign
like far bird voices, guesses
at exotic works and caresses.

A clapper clanging her bell of a body,
words harshly glad
with tonal sense strange, dialect-ravelled
mad as the rain
hiss . . . "Go on! travel!"
But in that darkness blotted with shapes
she must invent her destination,
while each time thunder tumbles
around her earlobes
the letters on the signboard jumble.

ONLY A RECESSION

After hunger
two days long,
sitting happy before
a plate of beans,

I delicately slit
each kernel with
my incisors,

let my tongue run
twitching with joy
across the texture
of the meat.

NATURE

As the orange-
striped cat
hunches,
glaring down,

the pale-fluffed
nestlings
he's discovered
feel cooled
in the shadow,

and

stretch their thin
necks, heavy
heads up,
hungry
beaks open,

wide
on hinges.

WEEK IN FRENCH CANADA

Two kids playing, singing around
their grinning, dripping baby;
for three days they were happy.

Then came that national institution,
the aunt with her voice whooping
from her barrel of a corset
and rage thick as her constitution.

Drained by those allies, TV
and clam-faced priests,
of the whole content of what is human,
what's left but a beast's pulse
tormenting a cavity in her cranium?

Now hear the baritone sacraments
and whole church inventory.
Oh you can tell she's Catholic,
but from what seminary?

The boy growls hot responses
for her prayers against neighbours,
and the girl mainly rebels
when she croons and tells her baby
secret thoughts with a singular fervor.

I SHOUT LOVE

I shout Love in a land muttering slack damnation
as I would in a blizzard's blow,
staggering stung by snowfire in the numbing tongues of cold,
for my heart's a furry sharp-toothed thing
that charges out whimpering
even when pain cries the sign written on it.

I shout Love even tho it might deafen you
and never say that Love's a mild thing
for it's hard, a violation
of all laws for the shrinking of people.
I *shout* Love, counting on the hope
that you'll sing and not shatter in Love's vibration.

I shout Love . . . Love . . . It's a net
scooping us weltering, fighting for joy
hearts beating out new tempos against each other.

The wild centre life explodes from a seed
recreates me daily in your eyes' innocence
as a small ancient creature, Love's inventor,
listened to a rainbow of whispers.

I shout Love against the proverbs of the damned
which they pause between clubbings and treacheries
to quote with wise communicative nods . . . I know
they're lies, but know too
that if I declared a truce in this war
they'd turn into pronged truths and disembowel me.

By what grim structure in the skull
do you justify unloveliness? I tell you
this machine has masters
who play their contradiction of music on you.

I shout Love against my prison where unconscious joy
like a brown sparrow chirping hoppity zig-zag
seems my keeper . . . In his bright ignorant eye
I live a prisoner while masons plonk stone
to soak up sunlight meant for prisoners
each one a piece of my brain, fragment of my heart's muscle.

And prisoners with hunger aching like a tooth in the belly;
              All the robbed ones —
wonderless kids,
     strengthless men,
          women with no vision for their womb-thoughts.
How'll I escape? Clang shut my own cell door?

I shout Love for all the colors and shapes of men,
all their subleties *
of blood and bone, thought and vision:
imagining for each
a destiny according to his particular beauty.

I shout Love for the womanflower, the manflower,
and don't too carefully tend them.
Inventing themselves moment by moment
out of joy, sorrow
and stark machinery of need,
what do they need of me before my truth?

I shout Love . . . which is just the beginning:
Truth . . . which is just the beginning:
Honor . . . which is just the beginning:
And sometimes turn from the long-fanged enemy
to eat the worm in my own heart.

Louis Riel, that man sad with wisdom
I Love . . . and his hope Canada:
for hopes are the taller parts of men,
my stilts and eyes' loving perspective,
hope my liver pumping the bile that is life.

*"subtleties" of course. But the misprint alone is worth the price!

66

Does anyone know where the corpse is buried?
Under whose stuffed seat? What dancer's foot?
Louis Riel I Love;
but the hangman drives to a Sunday picnic with his family
and whatever the martyr gained he claims.

Even I shout Love who aged ten thousand years
before my tenth birthday
in shame, wrath, and wickedness;
shout and grow young as cowards grow old:
Shout Love whom this world's paradoxical joy
makes stammer or keep silent between shoutings,
more held each hour by the wonder of it.

I shout You my Love in a springtime instant
when I wince half pain half joy to notes from an oriole
over balls of frost trapped in quickening roots,
and the tick-tock-tickle of warm rain
trickling into buds' eyes, plucking them open.

I shout Love into your pain when times change and you must change:
minutes seeming final as a judge's sentence
when skies crack and fall
like splinters of mirrors
and gauntle'd fingers, blued as a great rake,
pluck the balled yarn of your brain:

For Love's the spine holding me straight,
the eye in back of my shoulderblades *
that sees and beats my heart for all thinkers,
and the touch all over and thru me
I've often called God.

The herring with his sperm makes milk of the wide wrinkling
        wriggling ocean
where snowy whales jump rolling among whitecaps
as I shout live your Love and the deeds of my words
pollinate the air you're breathing.
Since life's a dream garment hung singing or sighing on a bone tree
why shouldn't it be Love's adventure?

*Or as Harry Gulkin once said "That secret finger up your..."

I shout Love between your knees that are my wings my Love,
when I ride like a dragon
blessing you fierce as curses.
Oh take me Love for I'm a storm of light
enwhorled with satanic darkness.

I whisper Love into the ear of a newborn girl,
breathing Love in her name.
May she grow up around her name singing inside her.

I shout Love against Death, that rattling, stinking harvest machine
that loves best the ripest and richest in Love.
I've seen their eyes bright with hunger
gorging on their last light;
and felt Love lurch sidling away
from the small help they wanted.

I shout Love and am no sentimentalist
but I* rejoice in the deaths of rogues.

But Love life thrilling roots
like nerves digging and* buried corpse,
the old fierce eye rotted and born new,
an enemy lost in a lover.

I shout Love wherever there's loveless silence;
in dumb rocks, in black iron lie oppressed minds
like parsecs of night between the stars,
where suns in tumultuous sleep toss eruptions about them
and I wake with a cry
spinning among the galaxies.

I shout Love to the young whose eyes are clouded with light
as their light clouds my eyes.
Only as beards of wheat swaying at the fingertips may I touch them
for they're born in the centre, are the centre,
and I shout Love, even tho
there's something of me they must destroy.

*"for"
*"the"

You to whom honor came so easily
in your darling girl world,
when your joy changed so quickly to defiance
you shocked us but
you made our hearts and brains beat one rhythm
and we followed you.

I shout Love at those grey-lipped men who trim life:
Shout Love into their dim ears, their shaking heads.

I Love the dawn, with a half-risen sun rosy like the head of God's
        phallus.

But what if I came shouting Love now
to you shivering in your blanket
unfed for forty-eight hours?
The liberals goggle over their cocktails
to talk patiently of feeding you,
but I shout Love and I mean business.

I shout Love in those four-letter words
contrived to smudge and put it in a harmless place,
for Love today's a curse and defiance.
Listen you money-plated bastards
puffing to blow back the rolling Earth with your propaganda
        bellows and oh-so-reasoned negations of Creation:
When I shout Love I mean your destruction. *

   *A revision is
"When should I shout love
I mean the end
Of you
As you are."

69

ORDINARY STORY

What maddens me? Listen:
there was greyeyes
eleven-twelve, tall
bony and strong-rumped,
with her little sister browneyes
(their clothes brown
poverty-brown with
straight-banged mother-haircuts).
It was browneyes' birthday
and greyeyes took her
out on the street
to ask a present
from strangers.

Hold on, browneyed poet!
It was likely
a story, but a good one;
and browneyes could hardly speak
with wanting. Needed coaching
from greyeyes, strong
desprit but in command
and in a grim way warm
like a U-boat captain
or Ruski Christ harrowing
Hell in a 57-ton tank.
A good dimesworth story!

What maddens me is
greyeyes' future, always
strong, a little bitter but
not letting it spoil the fun
or her love, strong, decisive.
One night deliberately
leaving her pants home;
and then the ordinary story
of a man with job-wounded hands,

tired, tender
only in bed, or
on the sweet end of Sunday.

Ordinary . . . Yet
I rave and like a Samson
poke at the keystone of the world
in desprit hope
that greyeyes' life
won't be at all
ordinary.

VIEW FROM A TIME MACHINE

The age of adventure
isn't done; in Toronto
a tugboat captain was

(the green rolling hips
of waves, his love
and his support
were girdled
by ice pale as steel
and snow hissing in flight)

broke by medical expenses
and the bailiff came
to give his wife and child
(both ill) new quarters
on the sidewalk.

This being an age
(space flight for example)
of adventure,
he stood guard
with a shotgun.

KNOWING I LIVE IN A DARK AGE

Knowing I live in a dark age before history, *
I watch my wallet and
am less struck by gunfights in the avenues
than by the newsie with his dirty pink chapped face
calling a shabby poet back for his change.

The crows mobbing the blinking, sun-stupid owl;
wolves eating a hamstrung calf hindend first,
keeping their meat alive and fresh . . . these
are marks of foresight, beginnings of wit:
but Jesus wearing thorns and sunstroke
beating his life and death into words
to break the rods and blunt the axes of Rome:
this and like things followed.

Knowing that in this advertising rainbow
I live like a trapeze artist with a headache,
my poems are no aspirins . . . they show
pale bayonets of grass waving thin on dunes;
the paralytic and his lyric secrets;
my friend Al, union builder and cynic,
hesitating to believe his own delicate poems
lest he believe in something better than himself:
and history, which is yet to begin,
will exceed this, exalt this
as a poem erases and rewrites its poet.

*This is considered a take-off from Brecht. Actually we both got it
from Engels.

IDYL

Hooray for the farmer,
aching backbone of the country.
Bless him he's got more things to fix
and less to fix them with
than anybody,
and talk about early rising

Why at 5 a.m. he's woke up by
a bloody ignorant calf bawling in his ear
and before city folks are awake
he's tearing along the highway,
sixty miles an hour
on one damn errand or another.

He's got two-three times as much land
and two-three times fine shingly ruins
(good kindling) and owns
a TV, a truck, a tractor,
and maybe one wife
somewhat less mechanized.

Oh prosperous free enterprise
that replaces two blades of grass
with two and a half, five
husky devils with one, and
leaves him all their worries.

YOU GROWING

You growing and your thought threading
the delicate strength of your focus,
out of a clamor of voices,
demanding faces and noises,
apart from me but vivid
as when I kissed you and chuckled:

Wherever you are be fearless;
and wherever I am I hope to know
you're moving vivid beyond me,
so I grow by the strength
of your fighting for your self, your life. *

   *Revised to:
"...your self, many selves, your life, many lives...your people."
More a clarification of meaning than a change.

JANUARY SPARROW

Two rusty wires jammed rubbing
make music in January. Look up
and on a wire between two snow-tufts
a grey puff of a sparrow's
fluffed warm in this dank wind.

January Armstrong *
make the air cringe again
with a song come via your gearbox larnyx
from a heart big as a diesel engine!

*Louis Armstrong: American Black singer, with a raspy voice so bad
it was good.

CHESS

A creation, but once the substance
was given pattern, painted
the colors of night, manbone and blood,
sculpted into men with sure powers,
it acquired its own laws, moves
and their effects having nothing
to do with its creator's tinted vision.

Yet the tool, the vision's needed
in the mindseye of the player, the
reflection of squares and mock men
moving, building the concept which
must have truth and its own growth
or be shattered on the cruel board.

What's fatal isn't the vision but
confusion of vision with the hard board,
the feel of godhead manipulating
men according to exact fancy, to
miss or with fine passion deny
the relentless laws, the powers of men.

74

REQUEST

Be young . . . Walk impudently humming
— hair a lemon cloud inlaid with sunset,
between ridges of my brain.

I'm all torn murk and lightning
— stink with blood of crocodiles I've wounded.
Be young . . . Have eyes a sun-leached sky
where swallows whiz in parabolas.

Let a shy hand find your woman hair,
the wee mouth at your breast
be like your chuckle in the bell of my skull
— young, possessed.

IN THIS GAME THERE NEEDS TO BE NO LOSERS

The glinting long and faintly blue bayonet's a gun's tongue
and drinks sweet wine
tho it owns no thirst or malice,
nor do our rockrough millstones of moons and planets
taste the human grain falling, falling
a faint mist of powder
into dark wind. No man's joy
ought to make hate or fate in this game
. . . there needs to be no losers.

But jokers are tossed in like clubs
ripped green off trees dripping acid,
hilts of weapons arbitrary
with weight and motion stuck into urgent hands
on the do-or-don't spot, balls pitched wary
with malice while the people-pebbled stands cry
"The Umpire! The Umpire! Believe in the Umpire!"

and Dad says, "You'll come to a bad end
if you don't heed the Umpire!"
and Mom says, "I'm sorry, there *is* an Umpire!"
and the Umpire yells
"If your eye gets too gleamy, blink it
or you'll see too bright to look, walk, talk past
the losers! There's got to be losers!"

"In this game there needs to be no losers":
Ike Strange, straight as a runner's thighbone
and arrogant with love, said this
standing at a bank-marble-sharpened corner
while dank air blew men about . . .
but didn't the wind from his lips
twist me round my pain? and
couldn't that smart buck-toothed accountant
Death, mumble a hardly felt obscenity
and put me down, a few red squigs on the page?
Still I've watched him play, seen him
a secret dreaming on his sharp face
and all his cards turned down, each one
in turn blessed with a touch, a look, a toss
(diamond, spade, fool, hanged man, lover's chariot)
onto the green table . . . So long
as he guessed the card his own he'd play it.

In this game there needs to be no losers . . . I know
the desiccated skins of losers
whisper and rattle past
in every switch of breeze; know
their glue-dim eyes and blasted wishes
tug me to join their flutter: but
in this game there needs to be no losers
tho nearly all lose . . . I know
my first trump of a yell and heart's jump dealt me in
to muse at my soul's strange faces, and wonder
how chances flow from hand to hand
in this game where there needs to be no losers
and I play my mauled, rainbeaten pack
plus near three billion others, all to win.

Once in a nice little country where people were a bit old-fashioned but nevertheless got along with each other quite well, considering, there was a Jewish boy named Daniel and our story begins on the eighth day of his life, when he was circumcised. Instead of the expected wail his relatives heard a gurgle of joy - - - precocious in one his age - - - come from the child. No wonder. Freed from the foreskin's restraint the loveliest pair of little wings unfolded upon the head of Daniel's dingus, and giving them all little time for surprise the dingus at once took off and fluttered somewhat awkwardly about the synagogue, chirping notes already showing signs of musical promise. When it grew tired the dingus returned to its natural perch. Only then did his uncle find presence of mind enough to sigh, "Oh it's hard to be a Jew!" as he was supposed to, but Daniel didn't look the least bit sad.

In that nice little country there was no such place as a ghetto but all the Jews lived together in one end of town and everybody thought it was just as well. The town wasn't very big - - - the country wasn't very big and this wasn't even the capital - - - and the end of town where the Jews lived opened up onto the countryside. There were woods with rabbits and squirrels, meadows with flowers and cows, haystacks, hedges, birds singing almost everywhere.

Daniel's parents were the kind of people that people who were very poor called rich, and getting richer, but still were friendly with almost everybody and not too much set on their dignity. So in the first three or four years during which almost anything a child can do is considered delightful Daniel and his winged dingus were more or less unrestrained. In fact the two, but especially the winged dingus, were causes of wonder and joy to all the Jews in that pretty little town in the nice little country.

The sight of Daniel's dingus fluttering around his head or perched there with wings pretty as a butterfly's stretched out, looking almost like a bow in his hair, while he trotted about on his small concerns, was charming. More often, since it was a good little dingus - - - just as Daniel was a good little boy - - - it hung in its proper place; but there were times when it wandered into the fields, watched the birds fly, listened to them sing, learned to sing and fly as well as the best of them. Often in the early morning it would be especially rambunctious, streak out of Daniel's open window, fly higher and higher till it was circling quite out of sight, singing like a lark.

This latter activity went on all one summer, and even thru the fall, but when winter came with its dark and its doubts, the people, especially Daniel's parents, began to consider. Besides Daniel was reaching the age when the doings of boys and their dinguses begin to be considered more annoying than amusing. Daniel was beginning to look a little man and even if the time was still pretty far off the thought of a real man with a dingus so much more than usually out of control as was Daniel's was sobering. What if the winged dingus led him to being involved with a gentile girl? Even in such a nice little country such a thing would be disturbing, in more ways than one.

There was no conference of elders upon the subject --- this was during one of those periodic advanced and modern ages --- but everybody agreed on what had to be done, and in fact Daniel's parents were among the first to agree. The winged dingus was tied up, fastened to a leash with the end looped around Daniel's waist, and for the next ten years or so everybody did their best to forget about it. As time went on such small evidences of waywardness as had shown in Daniel's character disappeared. He went into his father's business, left for work early every morning, in general showed a singleminded attention to duty.

Now the nice little country had a king, and the king had a daughter the same age as Daniel but --- in spite of Daniel's fine face and figure --- much better looking. All the citizens of the nice little country said they loved her. So did the young unmarried kings of the nasty cold northern country to the north and the nasty hot southern country to the south of the nice little country --- or at least their respective ministers of foreign affairs said the young kings loved her. She was the only heir.

When she was about fifteen years old and everybody asserted she was very beautiful --- which actually was no lie --- the princess went on a tour of the nice little country; here and there, back and forth, for almost a week till she'd seen every part of it. She came to the pretty little town where Daniel lived, and Daniel saw her. Their eyes met. Two electric currents, one from each of her eyes, shot across and into Daniel's eyes; from there they travelled down, one by way of his stomach, one along his backbone: and when they met and fused at the bottom the winged dingus fluttered like mad.

It had become so tame, hung so long and so meekly, forgetting even its sweet songs, that it had ceased to distract Daniel from concerns important in the world. But now the winged dingus sang more wondrously than ever, darted and jerked against its leash, causing Daniel to feel spasms of joy so intense he was almost terrorized. It wanted to be let go, to play games with the swallows and the dragonflies, to sail up into the sky, piebald with clouds, looking for adventure; and it promised Daniel such wonder if this were done (and it was such a pain to keep it tied) that after half a day of struggling with his conscience Daniel undid the leash. The winged dingus shot off into a dusk blue as thin smoke.

In the morning it was back, chirping softly to him of doings he could barely understand, but filling him with content and wondrously colored daydreams. From then on the winged dingus was away every night. Daniel was happy, but didn't go to work so early in the morning. His interest in the business declined.

That winter an awful rumor trickled from mouth to ear, from taproom to parlor, throughout the nice little country. The princess, the lovely and innocent looking princess, was in that condition which cynics say is much more interesting to observe than to endure.

Indeed it was the truth. Physicians confirmed it. The king's most inward of inner councils sat in a fog of dismay, and the princess was urgently invited to attend. She was flattered till she found out what was the subject of the meeting. Then she was puzzled; didn't know exactly what she'd done, or what she was expected to do about it.

"You've spoiled our whole foreign policy for one thing!" thundered the king, pounding his mace on the table, "Here we were trying to decide whether to marry you to the king of the nasty cold northern country and go to war with the nasty hot southern country, or else marry you to the king of the nasty hot southern country and go to war with the nasty cold northern country. Now we can't go to war with anybody because we can't marry you to anybody. You're a ruined young lady!"

When she finally understood what it was they wanted her to tell, the princess said why yes she'd tell. . . . But added that she didn't know what it was about it that seemed so disastrous because the whole thing was quite nice, in fact sensationally nice, something that ought to happen to any young girl about her age, or at least to any princess. Then she told of the bird with lovely wings who came to her chamber at night, and how it sang to her more sweetly than she'd ever before been sung to, and all the wonderful rest of it.

That night the king and the whole of his inwardest inner council kept watch behind the curtains in the princess' chamber. They saw the winged dingus come and heard its song, but waited still. You see they didn't believe the princess' story, and wanted to see who had trained this wonderful bird, and when he would come. So they waited while everything else happened too. In the morning the winged dingus flew out the window, and they all realized that what the beautiful princess had told them was true.

"Call the royal falcon!" cried the king, waving his sword.

So the royal falcon, fierce and dutiful, set out in pursuit of Daniel's winged dingus; and the winged dingus fled before him. The dingus tried straight-out flight, but the falcon was faster. It ducked into clouds, but sooner or later it would have to duck out, and there the falcon would be waiting for it. It flew high, flew low, led the falcon a wild chase thru forests and mountain canyons. Actually it had a merry time, for never once in the whole flight did it think that anything as joyous and innocent as itself could be overcome. But it was caught, and that was the end of it. The baby, to save it trouble in life, was aborted.

Daniel had a shock when the winged dingus didn't come back, brooded a little because it never did come back; but he got over it, started going to work earlier than ever in the morning, learned the business better than his father ever had, and before too long --- as time goes --- was a very rich man. As for the princess she got over it or didn't get over it, depending on how you look at things. She never married either, but didn't let that cramp her style. In fact after her father died and left her the kingdom she soon ran it into debt with her extravagant habits. So Daniel and the princess did meet finally, if not as bride and groom at least as moneylender and client. Daniel came to practically own the nice little country after a while, and managed to arrange a war with someone or other after all. The nice little country was victorious, with the help of some ally or other, and became not quite so little. . . . Not quite so nice either.

So nearly everybody lived, not so happily and not ever after either, but at least they lived for a while, and that's something.

THE RED AND GREEN PONY

Tommy found the red and green pony in the place of the dream, where there were no shadows because the air itself was the light, and swirled about him with its butterflies as he walked, his knees touched by grass gentle with pollen. He was headed towards the trees. In that place he always headed towards the trees. The leaves were like tongues and spoke things that tickled on the inside of his ears. Things he never understood, although he listened hard.

This time he got closer to the trees than he ever had before. He passed a last roll in the land and there in a hollow beneath the first of them --- a tall one, flowering like a dogwood --- was the red and green pony, busy as a lawnmower at the grass.

The pony was red and green, not in patches but all over. You saw both colors at once. That's how Tommy knew it wasn't real. But real or no it looked up and into Tommy's eye, chewing as it did, while he walked straight at it.

"Look out, red and green pony," said Tommy, "I'm going to walk right through you."

"That's the best trick I ever heard of," said the red and green pony. "Can you do it?"

"I can," said Tommy, "because you're red all over and green all over --- Two colors all the same time. That proves you aren't really real."

"Well you're pink all over and noisy all through," said the red and green pony, "and still you're real."

It turned sideways to Tommy and started to work on the grass again. It looked so convincing that Tommy stopped just short and put his hand out to touch. The hair part was silky but tangled, the pony part solid as the side of a house.

"You feel real," said Tommy, "but your hair needs combing." He was indignant at this intrusion in his dream --- the only place he was let be his own --- half curious.

"Next time you come in my dream," said the red and green pony, "bring a comb, and a hairbrush too."

Tommy took two steps back and got mad. "This isn't your dream. It's my dream, and you aren't real because you're in it, and if you don't look out I'll toss you out of it."

The red and green pony faced Tommy hard, not mad, but standing on its rights. "Your dream or mine," it said, "try tossing and see if I'm not real." All of a sudden the dream closed in around them both. There were no more trees, no swirling light; only Tommy, the red and green pony, and a little grass.

Tommy knew he could turn some dreams his way if he twisted them hard: but never before one of these bright ones. He liked the red and green pony; but here, where it was most beautiful and most his, he couldn't stand it. He looked hard and made the twist in his mind that sometimes works in dreams.

Next instant the ground jerked out from under him like a rug, he was looking at his legs kicking and spinning above him. The red and green pony called something after him, and then the dream was gone. It was half-light --- not early dawn, the day was dull although it was summer, and he was lying in bed. But he remembered what the red and green pony had called to him, "When you come back remember to bring a comb and a hairbrush," and he wasn't unhappy. He knew he was coming back.

Meantime it was day and not as bright as the dream.

✦2

Days were never like the bright dreams. Inside Tommy where his heart hurried up the seconds there was brightness. Like the airy light of the dream it swirled, and carried him with its swirls. Sometimes he tried to make the day as bright as the dream; but it had a frustrating will of its own and wouldn't be.

He dressed, straightening his laces to please, and went downstairs. The kitchen was neat. He'd never gotten up so early that the kitchen wasn't neat. A pin on the floor would have been as conspicuous as an anchor.

His father and mother were having breakfast there. His father was reading the paper.

81

"CCF's running a candidate here again," said his father. "Are they ever going to learn that we here in Ontario don't want them?"

"I guess they ought to," said his mother.

"Yanks kicking up a fuss about Negroes going to white schools again," said his father. "Why can't they just explain the situation logically to the Negroes instead of all this rioting?"

But his mother was a mother and knew Tommy was in the room. Her eyes looked him over and inventoried his parts. "Did you wash?" she asked.

Tommy didn't say a word, just started towards the sink. "Don't you know better than to wash there? Go upstairs to the proper place!" This was his father.

Tommy planted one heel ahead of him and pivoted round on it. This was a ritual. If he'd washed in the bathroom they'd tell him he hadn't used the right towel. If he'd used the right towel . . .

He looked at his father and saw his gaze was like a policeman's at a dog without a license. Suddenly, in spite of what would happen, the brightness inside him flared: "You know I had a dream and saw a red and green pony!" It came all in a burst.

His father's hard look gathered a smile around it. "That's nice . . . But you know of course a pony can't be red and green. It may be red and white in patches, but even then the red is more like . . ."

"But I saw it," said Tommy.

"Certainly you saw it," said his father --- he could unbend, within due limits of course, at times, "but it was in a dream. Now did you ever see a pony on the street with red and green patches?"

"But this was different. It was red all over and green all over!"

His father's paper came down with a rustle and thump. "Young man, don't tell lies!"

"Now George," said his mother weakly, "don't be too hard on him again . . . It was only his dream."

"You don't understand dear," said his father. "He's got to realize there are things that can't be. If you allow him dreams like that there's no telling what he'll be wanting next." His eyes turned to the boy again:

"Tommy, even in a dream such things can't be. It's impossible to see two colors in the same place at the same time." He smiled as if settling the subject, "Now tell me honestly . . . You didn't really see a red and green pony, did you?"

"Why not?" cried Tommy. "Aren't I pink all over and noisy all through?"

"Tommy!" This time it was his mother. "Where did you ever get such indecent thoughts? You don't talk about your insides, Tommy!"

"Things can't be made to suit your foolish fancies, Tommy," said his father. "Now go upstairs and wash. We'll talk about it later."

He was picking up the newspaper when Tommy left.

"Now they even want to interfere with my dreams!" whimpered Tommy to himself upstairs. He washed and then looked out the window at the bumpy crumple-paved street; at the river with its sign: "Warning. No swimming or fishing. Water Polluted. Order of Ontario Department of Health." The water was pale and poisonous-looking, like restaurant soup. The light was dull, as if shining through ashes, and unlike the dream-light it had shadows.

It turned out he was scolded for letting his breakfast get cold, and the red and green pony was forgotten. But when Tommy went to sleep that night he put a comb under his pillow.

✳3

"Tommy! Tommy!" the leaves said.

No, on second listen, it wasn't his name the leaves were saying. It was something strange, something he'd maybe known once and then forgotten. He opened his eyes and let the light of the dream swirl into them.

He was lying right where he'd left the dream before, the flowered branches, the tufts of the grass, swinging over him like pony-tails. The comb was in his hand but he hadn't brought the hairbrush. He got up and the red and green pony was there . . . a tiny image of Tommy in each of its looking eyes.

"What's your name, red and green pony?" said Tommy.

"My name's Red And Green Pony, with capital letters. Did you bring the comb?"

"Yes," said Tommy, and started to comb the hair on the pony's sides --- a sweet-smelling dust came up as the teeth pulled through the tangles. "My father said you couldn't be, because that'd suit my foolish fancies."

A dragon-fly came skating along a diagonal of the breeze, and settled on the pony's back. Tommy was going to knock it off but it settled its wings and looked like it belonged there. Later it flew away. "Your father means everything should suit his own fancies, foolish or not, and no one else's," said the red and green pony.

"Oh, my father doesn't believe in foolish fancies," said Tommy, "all he believes in are good solid facts."

"Everybody has their own good solid facts," said the red and green pony, "and usually they're the foolishest fancies of all."

Suddenly, in a small place near Tommy's heart, something nice exploded and spread all through him. "I'm glad you're in the dream," he said, "and if you say it's your dream I'll let it be."

"Let's both say it's the dream's dream," said the red and green pony, "and if we let it be its own dream then it'll be ours. That's the rule."

"That's a funny rule," said Tommy. "What happens if we don't let it be its own dream?"

83

"Then it's its own dream anyway, but not ours."

Tommy stuck the comb in the pony's mane, which was red all through and green all through, only paler, and put his arms around its neck, "Then I'll let you be your own Red And Green Pony," he shouted in love and triumph. "So you're mine!"

"Then get on my back," said the red and green pony.

They rode into the woods. The voices of the leaves grew louder, more ticklish in his ears, but still Tommy couldn't make out exactly what they were saying. The light here was greenish mixed with streams of purple that sometimes touched the pony's mane and slid down through it. There were still no shadows. "Let's talk about important things," said the red and green pony.

"Important" was when the fat on grown-ups' faces became cut up by lines and looked hard. Tommy couldn't think of anything important about himself so he told important things about his father . . . How he was a foreman and tried to keep that damned Communist shop steward in his place; how he belonged to the Orange Lodge and went the second Wednesday night of each month to condemn the Catholics. Somehow he felt he was saying the wrong things.

Then the red and green pony talked about its important things . . . Things so strange and of a different kind of importance that Tommy tugged at its mane and asked if those things were really true.

"True as there's three moons in the sky and they're playing leapfrog," said the red and green pony. And Tommy looked up through a gap in the trees and saw it was so.

Then they went past right under a bough and as they did the lowest branch bent down and whispered in his ear, "Tommy." It was as if he'd never heard his name before: as if he'd just been born and someone wise with stars whirling like fireflies around his head had stooped down and whispered his name into his inner ear, and the name had become him.

Again he tried to listen to what else the leaves were saying, but the dream had come to an end, and there it ended.

A starling was hopping about on his window-sill, almost in his room. It looked at him out of one eye, then out of the other, and he almost had his hand on it before it flew away. Down by the polluted river the green-grey leaves of a willow were in rustling motion. The day was bright and intricate, ugliness coiled with beauty.

✤4

Two aspects of life don't always compete. One can enrich the other. Tommy decided it was only fair for the red and green pony to have a share in the day as well. So the pony appeared, not exactly seen --- in fact if Tommy had been pressed he'd have had to admit that now the red and green pony was only imagined --- but it was there. All this could have gone for the best, but the day was its own day, and things went as they chose.

Tommy and the red and green pony made a game between them. First Tommy would show the pony something and then the pony would show something to Tommy. If nerve was called for, each would encourage the other not to be nervous: though actually the pony was very brave, and didn't need so much encouragement.

"Don't be scared of old Bumbly," said the red and green pony. "He's only going about his business." Told that, Tommy wasn't scared, and watched the bumblebee on its heavy, blustering flight. Watched how the devil's paintbrush bent, struggling like a wrestler in a full-nelson, while the bee bullied its way through the petals.

Tommy showed the red and green pony the willow tree by the polluted river, and how its leaves were always in motion, like a pretty lady in a shower-bath. Then he forgot the rule and asked, "What are those leaves saying, Red And Green Pony?"

"Now that's a silly unscientific question if I ever heard one," said the rep and green pony. "You know it's only our own personal leaves that talk."

"What do our own personal leaves say, Red And Green Pony?"

"Tommy!" No, it wasn't a whisper. It was his mother's long-drawn, treaclish imitation of an affectionate summons. He looked up. The thin waves of the polluted river lapped almost at his feet. The sun was on the down-slide of the sky. The day had gone.

"Tommy, where are you? Your father's home."

"Now why should she mention that special?" Tommy asked the imaginary red and green pony. "He's always home for supper."

He got no answer. The imagination pony was gone. Tommy couldn't summon up belief enough even to say goodbye.

"Tommy, what were you doing by the river? Do you want to catch a disease?"

"Yes, mother," said Tommy, not having heard the question, really. His father was there, standing with his mother on the lawn in front of the house. "Now George . . . Don't be too hard on him," said his mother.

"Young man," said his father, "your mother tells me you've been behaving strangely, talking out loud to yourself, playing by the river. Is it true?"

"Maybe."

"What do you mean maybe? And call me Father."

"I was playing a game," said Tommy, and stuck one heel in the ground, half wishing to pivot around on it. "Father . . . I mean."

"Tommy, didn't I tell you you couldn't give way to foolish fancies? What sort of game were you playing?"

"Just a game," said Tommy. "What's for supper?" He wasn't a bit hungry.

Then his father said one of those things that seemed to strip Tommy bare naked with one terrible rip, "It was your Red And Green Pony, wasn't it? Don't lie to me!"

"George!" cried his mother, in genuine shock, for this was a blow at her too. "There's nothing wrong with Tommy's mind! Don't you suggest such a thing!" But Tommy didn't hear, didn't care, the whole world and sky was rocking, chunks falling about him. His father had him trapped, could make him admit the Red And Green Pony was only imaginary.

Then he yelled, "There is a Red And Green Pony! You spell it with capital letters! It's red all over and green all over!" He pivoted on that heel and started to run.

"Tommy, come back! It's time for supper!" cried his mother.

"Let him go," said his father. "He's got to come back."

Then Tommy heard no more. He had run too far away.

✦5

"Tommy! Tommy!" He lay hidden not far from home, in a piney patch here on the edge of town where the limbs were ragged and thick like cloud-banks. His heartbeats shook his stomach and every beat was a wave of blackness.

"Tommy! Tommy!" It was his mother calling him, the sound trying to force itself into him through his ears. Sometimes it reached him and he half-caught his breath to answer, but another of those waves would sweep through him and choke off the word unsaid. Time was passing and through the westward branches he could see the sun, low and red. Time was going faster, the trees making strange noises.

"There is a Red And Green Pony," he whispered to himself, and wept.

He rolled half-over and there was a bug, small and with a longish, jointed body, short legs and feelers, climbing up a grass-stem. Suddenly a long-legged wolf spider pounced and the two toppled, hooked together by the spider's legs, to the ground. Tommy watched while the spider squatted over its victim, saliva pouring from its jaws, making a drop in which the creature's struggles weakened.

Tommy wept for the bug, but didn't touch the spider. It was fierce and had authority. Suddenly spider and bug were gone, lost as if blown out in the swirl of the airy light. A wave of warmth and happiness swept over Tommy. He looked up.

"Did you bring the hairbrush?" said the red and green pony. "The comb was nice but now I need a hairbrush."

"What do you want a hairbrush for?" asked Tommy.

"Why to brush hair, naturally," said the red and green pony.

"Well I've got it, Red And Green Pony," said Tommy, and he did have it.

"Tommy! Tommy!" He was brushing the pony's hair but someone kept calling him. No, two people. No, not them after all. He was out in the grass in the place of the dream and the voices of the leaves were calling to him, lonesome for him. There was a mixture, a conflict in the sound, that disturbed him. The air was a swirl in which the stems and tufts of the grass swung every which way. There were no flowers, but the butterflies were the flowers of the air, and one was perched on a grass-stem near him.

"Now I'm surely sure you're really real, Red And Green Pony," said Tommy, for he saw something even stranger. The patterns on the butterfly's wings were lines and swirls and figure-eights of color --- two three four colors seen running through each other, all seen in the same place.

"Tommy! Tommy!" No, this time he was sure it was his father and mother, but he was hiding from them. They kept him from hearing the leaves. "Take me on your back, Red And Green Pony," said Tommy. "I want to go to the woods."

"What are the leaves saying, Red And Green Pony?" he asked as the pony started to trot. "I think they're saying, 'Tommy', but there's something else."

"Don't listen so hard," said the red and green pony. "You've just got to let them say what they'll say."

Tommy listened, but all at once he imagined he heard his father and mother again. Imagined because they came into the dream like the pony came into the day, not really there. But though they weren't really there they seemed to be just ahead of them, standing in the grass, not angry but pleading and frightened.

"Look out, Red And Green Pony," Tommy cried. "You'll run those people down."

"Foo . . . Those people are just your imagination," said the red and green pony, and trotted right through them.

They came to the woods and the light was green, with streams of purple and other colors sliding through it . . . making tangles and sliding through each other. The leaves cried all around him, the words suddenly urgent and almost understood.

"Red And Green Pony, I think I hear what they're saying."

"Then listen," said the red and green pony. "To listen properly you've got to do it and not talk about it."

Tommy did listen. He listened for a long time, and understood. Only once more did he shake out of it and remember where he was, riding on the back of the red and green pony.

"Where are we going, Red And Green Pony?" he asked.

"All the way," said the pony. "Often and often you've got to go all the way so you can properly get back."

THE FLOWER OF MAN'S RESPONSE

It turned out the mattress the landlord'd promised me
was on another couple's bed. Furthermore
it was that bearded man himself who greeted me
and helped me carry it down. They hadn't
paid their rent and I had, so I slept well.

I'd gotten so used to the philosophical conclusion
that everything I had was taken from somebody else
that it didn't bother me at all to be faced with it
concretely; but still here, writing my poems
about the ultimate man, rising like a phallus
to every call for a response — emotional and brave
as all hell . . . I wonder if there's something about being human
        I'm not getting at.

HERE'S TO THE BOTTLE

Here's to the bottle I'm drinking
And here's to all the bottles I've drunk;
Rent a quarter-acre for my gravesite
and make a pyramid out of bottles,
Labels out . . .

Here's to my drinking companions
Even when I've drunk alone . . .
Rent an acre for my gravesite
And pile us all, soak us in alcohol
And make a special match,
A special engraved souvenir match
To strike a light

TO A COCKROACH

Itsel ting, thee gives me a big wish
for words in some wee chir-
ped language

Since in the shaaaaaaa-
dow of Earnie's foot, thee stopped
and thy feelers all flit-flutter
went swiftly *

not as if thee heared the high distractions
we bowled back and between us;
no — test-tastily thee
widdled the air, an so so so so

sharp thy wittle concern-things
touch-trembled thee . . . I see
how thee's got Earnie (old
bullet-in-the-brain-him Earnie) who

thee so pestify
all so absurdily tilted with love.

TEARS THE DEW OF BEAUTY'S MOURNING

Thinking of a dove I have never seen
— tobacco leaf feathers, incense smoke and cream,
Eyes that bob black walking, in startled take-off;
Circles those eyes describe in the flutter roar, whisper and whistle
Of wings — shadows and shadow colors of thought and the world:

That there is no mourning in the dove, not in its cry
Except in the thought of it there's the thought of tears
Tiny and plump, as things living, running down shadowed face flesh;
And in tears, especially quiet ones, all things take beauty's texture . . .

*"swiftly"

I've cursed death as the realest face of God
— black finger swallowing the buttercup, shadow deeper
Than all the underness of waves; in the tap of that finger
        . . . vanishment.
The priest in black and gold of all his robed belly
Threatened death as all the pain-grey flashes
Of the worst of life, as life continuous —
A scream in which the throat's continually torn, fragmented
        and reborn —

But when I was thirteen Confucius appeared in a quotation
And dream as two merry eyes over a beard like sun and moon
        over the woodsey world;
Saying: — "Not know life . . . How know death?" And silent
As a foetal smile his laugh has grown in what you might call my soul.

I've thought of death as an ambiguous flavor, the swiftest taste
Which dissolves as you wonder what it's like —
As light fleeing from the last star on the edge of the universe
Its curving wave-front as wings, no eyes behind,
No brother-light or thought of light in front, no thought;
As the tongue-lick of a purring lioness . . .

And conversely I've denied with less fear than I've denied
My oh-so-bragging, oh-so-punishing Lord, that death's ever more real
Than now when my atoms are showering about me
        popping like raindrops
— that my headstone exists, that any particular moment exists
Sitting like that stone atop my twin gems, serpent eyes
On the head of my patterned trail through time; that anything
        true now
Will still be true on any day in which I will not die.

And yet again I've thought, "I will die . . ."
No fear . . . The priest's threat was life, not death;
Survival of only part of me, my pain, survival of myself as pain
Only, and every part of me become pain, life
Screaming my wounded name forever and ever
As he had already made me scream it:
This is what I feared, and it's gone
Except in my negating laugh, a little gold flower
Plucked and falling over and over in light wind ripples . . .

In these days before any of Time's old unthought evils
Dies, it incarnates itself
In a human body, in a brain and spit-slurring tongue
To scheme and argue its eternity:
That there are evil men; that they are evil
May hurt the mind with its truth, but
I predict their deaths, not mine:
And this thought is my comfort —

No fear . . . But like a little patch of violet
On a calling dove's throat (some imaginary species)
Mourning . . . I've wept for myself
As a laughing child, like the son I've lost, all the lost children —
Pronouncing their names as they're pronounced on my home island:
Out of the mouth as out of a bell;
And the waves of a south blue sea have lapped the roots of my lashes
As if they were forested shores

AN AFFLICTED MAN'S EXCUSE

If all lights fell on me differently,
If the music differed, and the voices
Were others, perhaps I'd know better
Who I am: but now I can only guess it

Thru my refusals (like some one kind of person
Wonderful maybe, at least strange
Were going thru something like an orchard,
Picking up and throwing down). So many things

Of which I say, "Yes . . . I admire that!"
But what is it keeps me from folding
The whole dam basketfull of stars
Into my bosom? Why can't I give

My most personal love, which I've often said
Was universal, whenever it's asked? You need
Such a precise almighty balance with me
As to what you come on with, and what you hold back.

BRIGHT MOON

Bright moon. Oh if I could live like my spaniel
To whom all things are urgent and simple,
If not simple, nowhere: If my nerves drank my desires
As hers do . . . Maybe I could stick up one mysterious finger
And sign the moon as an artist might.

Description isn't for poets. Poetry demands an exactitude
That defies description. Liken the soul to an electron
, but when you say 'like' that implies 'not quite';
or drop that word: but then you're speaking of something else entirely
going on in the nucleus.

Like yesterday I told a man I loved him . . . And the delight,
The entire going with the necessity of my statement,
Made me ride the next hour like on a surfboard. Poor guy
: he disappointed me. But then . . . Why be disappointed?

You can smile at a Chinese like that. I've noticed that.
Sort of to say, "You're there . . . I'm here too . . . And
Isn't this a crusty cinder we walk on?" Dandelions I love
Because they grow where nobody wants them but the children,
The poets, and of course themselves.

"The moon is *not* a paper lantern," I told Roy,
"The moon's a big, jagged, dusty hunk of rock!"
He said, "It is to me." "Okay," I said, "make it a paper lantern
For me!" Which is a lie. It didn't go quite like that:
But similarly I liken the soul to an electron. Give it a charge
And it jumps to a new orbit. Therefore I praise the jump
Before it happens: Which makes the kids say I tell lies.
Well so I do . . . But my lies make things happen.

PROTESTING THE MURDER OF ERNEST HEMINGWAY

Hem you fink-out bastard! I'm yelling tears of hate
Against you . . . That house with a sonorous name
By the sonorous sea in a land with a sonorous leader;
Sonorous and brave and small, protected by its sonority
And resolve to live fully till death . . .

That house you left Forever To The People Of Cuba!
You could be there! You could be a symbol
Of defiance to the evil genius of your own land!

But no, Hem you cosmic quitter! Till the last
You had to be a Hemingway hero, like every one
Of your heroes except the last, that fisherman: —
Heroes whose names we can't remember, any more than
We remember the names of their complaisant women;
Treating their souls as reluctant visitors, setting conditions
Which had to be fulfilled before they accepted the duty
Of living for Mankind — Forever if possible.

THE BALLAD OF THE PINK-BROWN FENCE

Against the pink-brown fence with the sprucelet
My little sister stands to be photographed;
Fire tinges from her head and the dandelions —
Tear down the pink-brown fence to make a raft

Tear down the pink-brown fence to make a raft
Where my little sister stands to be photographed
Fish poke up their noses to make rings
And memories of dandelions dance from the ripples . . .

The camera is too slow to catch the gold
Of dandelions remembered around my little sister;
Stand up the old raft for a painting board
And guess the why of it — you can't recall kissing her . . .

Cut up the rotten painting for a bonfire;
The flames rush up a rattle, faint boom, and whisper;
Sparks fly gold in the night and then white;
Dandelions, and the hair of my little sister

RIDGWAY*BECOMES CHIEF OF STAFF

The defeated soldier gets a free trip
On a refrigerator ship;
His parents can console themselves with the notion
That defeat was really victory —
And partly to strengthen that illusion
The defeated general gets a promotion.

AS TRUE A LOVER'S KNOT

As true a lover's knot as the embrace of serpents green and gold,
Sweeter than the sting of their venom, lovelier than rattles in rhythm;
I would make with thee — swaying tall girl
Coming down from the hill with the orange groves
And the ruby sun thru your swinging long hair
Split up into tracks of rainbows . . .

The last long tongue of day's tasting the sea with lemon lights
                         and plum shadows
Between two mounts not so lovely as your breasts . . .
Naked as the air that kisses you, glistening with oil, perfume or dew
Or the distillation of your own sweet body,
My eye claims you, shall completely own this moment of you
Till a blow shall shatter it —

*As a matter of fact. It was Westmoreland.

94

And if you feel your skin mount into small nipples
As those nipples point themselves within the thrill of my gaze
I'll step out —
                    But with my eyes brownly lowered
So's you'll guess neither their color
Nor how much of your chosen life they allow
Which is their claim — the fiercest
A poet can make of a nude maiden . . .

But if my stilled tongue thrills itself to ask
It will be for all — no denial of my seed
When it quickens itself in yours
For my eye upon you claims the future; that
Thru time and all the tempers of the moon
There shall always be a damsel coming down from this hill
And her eyes and skin will be all the possibilities of colors
Now half sleeping, now half singing in you

THE CANADIAN STATUE OF LIBERTY SPEAKS
TO THE U.S. DRAFT DODGERS

Come to me you ones who are homeless at home
You insulted and sat on, enraged against your lazy wills —
I need two things: — skills and cheap labor
Plus unemployment to enforce the cheap labor:
So get a job and I will pass you; if you can't get a job, fake one!
But never, never ask for welfare; it is necessary for my system
                    that some people be completely desperate:
And though the local workers won't let you get away with that, with
                    you I have an excuse!

Just keep two things in mind: In this country as in yours we have a
                    rule of law
For the citizens of The State: And in this country even more
                    than yours

95

(Since we have never had a Revolution — the people's enforcement
of their law)
! THE STATE IS COMPLETELY LAWLESS!
Nevertheless I am generous: I have a rule
In my country you are free to talk, talk, talk all you like about your
rights;
As long as you don't start acting as if you *have* rights: —
I have rights! That's all boys!

IN VICTORY SQUARE

"Gerry! Gerry!" calls one tramp
to another. The chin
(flushed and dirty) beckons
peremptory as the voice
is meant to be; but the eyes

(are they black, suffused
as it were with the dust of pavements
, who can tell?) they plead,
and for that matter so does the voice

: for it's a matter of doubt if
Gerry will answer. Sure you
can take it for granted they've wet the mouth
of the same bottle (the man's call
with its garbagecan echoes, tells you that) n
number of times; but picture

what a bending down from an
unforgotten hope of dignity
any touch is down here, let alone
an acknowledgement of the things shared

implied in that call, desperate in its way
as the smallest things have come to be desperate
in my world as well as theirs.

PASSAGE TO HONG KONG

The British Ambassador passed over the bridge
From the side plastered with slogans about
                    The heart
                            The will
                                    The mind: —
To the side plastered with slogans
About
        The bowels
                    The breath
                            The tits . . .

It is said he finds the difference refreshing: —
Probably has money invested
in Bowel-Breath-Tit-Trust . . . . *

I'LL CAST A SILVER BULLET

I'll cast a silver bullet and bless it with my holiest kiss,
fire it just once and it'll rise
singing like a lark. Now and then it'll dive
down and delightedly thru the heart of one of those I hate.

Oh the "chirp-chirp-chirp" of its passing! Infants'll look up
and their eyes become drops of quicksilver at the thought that
        the world at last has a guardian
: and I, long since dead, will be at peace except in one of those
        moments
when it plunges and one more whorl of evil winks out

. . . then the watchers of my skeleton
will notice that for a moment my skull's grin
is a little broader.

*in the Bowel-Breath-Tit-Trust

97

WHERE IS CHE GUEVARA?

These are miraculous days . . . Worms sing! The sound
from their burrows is as lively as birds
but not so pleasant. And right now they are singing
"Where is Che Guevara?"

Che Guevara is beauty . . . The terrible and persistent
        beauty that's the end of those who can't stand it,
The end of worms.
They fear him and can't stop thinking of him.
The newspapers are speculating.
President Johnson busy breaking a treaty
As his forbears used to do on the Indians,
And now he does on the entire world
. . . . arranging the murder of a Vietnamese girl
three weeks old; pauses just an instant in the middle of
        handing out a souvenir pen
to think
        "Where is Che Guevara?"
"Who are the people who know?"
He can't tell . . . He's made too many enemies.

He has many agents but no friends,
Has had mistresses but no lovers;
And he who's often invoked God in support of ungodly lies
Wishes that God could exist for a moment
To answer one prayer . . . Tell him:
"Where is Che Guevara?"

I'll tell you where Che Guevara is . . . He moves.
He moves with the dead and unforgotten.
He moves with the lost Indians of the Pampas, hordes
        and hordes of them, tall on their horses.
He moves before their high lances, shining close-up like
        their burnished copper reins, invisible like those
        reins at a distance.
He moves.

He moves with Spartacus, up the Appian Way, blinking
        away the tears of memory and fixing two
        feelingly fierce eyes on Rome — Citadel of deceit,
        of the cannibals who devour men slowly . . . not
        their bodies but their entire lives.
And the time has come round . . . The time has come
        round for the end of it all;
So more importantly he moves with the living.

Oh you manipulators, you planners of sour lives and
        cheated deaths, you puppet masters
Who play with dolls who ache and grieve for the things
        you do to them in your playing,
Or perhaps you don't grieve any more, having forgotten or
        never known what living is like:
Did you not just now shiver violently
As if a tall seeming clumsy man in rubber boots clumped
        over your graves?
It is Che Guevara . . . He moves.
He moves precisely . . . He moves discretely.
He moves like the scalpel in the long bony hands of
        a great surgeon.
The cancer shall be cut out, and certainly the patient
        will survive.

Does he move as a little black dog, trotting everywhere,
        perhaps at the heels of an imperialist, sniffing
        them, holding in his guts the secret of how they
        shall be tripped?
No he moves by a more powerful magic than that.
Does he pass the frontier posts secreted in the womb
        of a pure virgin?
No he moves by a holier mystery than that.
He hates joyfully, he loves bitterly.
This is the fate of a man who is a man in this present age
And Che Guevara has not forsworn it.
There are others, millions of them, who also hate joyfully
        and love bitterly,
And they are his magic . . . They are his mystery.

Oh you putters and takers, you reckoners of dollars
        in the millions
— each digit of which is a piece of work, a piece of a life,
        usually a swindled piece:
Does conscience bother you? Or rather regret?
Do you think you have botched your lives?
And botched other peoples' lives even worse?
You students in Canadian Universities
Learning how to botch your lives
And botch other peoples' lives even worse:
Who are perhaps cynical, refusing to believe that a life
        can be anything but botched;
Or perhaps incapable even of understanding the concept
        of what is a life,
Really a life . . . Not botched:
Do you wonder "Where is Che Guevara?"
And does the thought make you unsteady, and do you
        clutch for support to the nearest lie to you?
Not the truth . . . That would be too awfully thrilling
        and demanding.
I tell you there are men on Earth who usually tell
        the truth
I know
Because I am one of them,
And know I'm not unique.

And I have chosen who I will believe
And what I will believe.
I have chosen to believe in the ultimate . . . the Loveliest
        thing I can imagine;
I have chosen to believe in You, not as you are
But as you should be . . . I believe in your happiest wishes!

                                        1965

THE FLOWERY MAN

(for J.C.)

Take a head off a tree and put it on a body
A head of blossoms with vines growing again
And while the human juices take over the graft
Educate among the bees, the Flowery Man.

Or take the man with two heads talking both ways
Internal heads that pop in place of the other;
He looks one way talking one side, one way talking the other
And screws of light go out from either gaze
One black and white in flashes
One different tints of greys:

The Flowery Man says: "Judge that you shall not be judged!"
If a sentimental stenographer gets it wrong
He's thinking of me and the two-headed one —
Our words jumble and cross as in a puzzle, like the
Doing-baby thinglings in an abstract song . . .

Where our two eyeflashes meet they bust into meteors
And other eyes light in the flash — flowers
Fold down into buds to reopen; and hours
Are hooked to play on the lines of the minutes

SCREAM A CREAM CONE

At that instant I heard the scream of this bubble of a
      universe
Or bubble on the universe in a conflagration of
      dimensions
— It's all the roaring ages' long scream of expansion — *

An artist in shorts squatted above me in a cage hung
            from the ceiling
Playing a board, stabbing the light with flashes of dark,
            the dark with injections of white fury
As his mates did, and other things — for what they
            had bandied and rolled about among their own
            yelling brains
Was not *what* I *should* see but that I should see some
            thing:

Between us the sparkle-eyed nervy unaged machine,
            alum-grey and like a clean page of fluctuating
            nothing,
Snatched away the sky like a sheet or a tablecloth
And the two worlds of Heaven and Earth tumbled and
      mixed ...

LIVE WITH ME ON EARTH UNDER THE
INVISIBLE DAYLIGHT MOON

Live with me on Earth among red berries and the
            bluebirds
And leafy young twigs whispering
Within such little spaces, between such floors of green,
            such figures in the clouds
That two of us could fill our lives with delicate wanting:

*Believe it or not a Black Mountain poet criticized this verse as
abstract. What can you say to a professional idiot?
I said it was concrete, because it had all the concrete in the world in it.

102

Where stars past the spruce copse mingle with fireflies
Or the dayscape flings a thousand tones of light back
    at the sun —
Be any one of the colors of an Earth lover;
Walk with me and sometimes cover your shadow with
    mine.

TONGUECUT PRINTS OF A CHILD MOUTH AS BIRDS

(To be read with windfire eyes)

The child singer in a cloud on the mountain
Troubles my thoughts of living things — their hearts, and roses
                                        pale-blue :
His smile's a mouth with wings beating stanzas like birds in flight —
Darkens and lightens with flying-out music . . .

Now his lips shape a gull wheeling across trapezoidal beams — the
                        sun drawing water
As fishermen say . . . drinking of its pool of tears
To cry again, with joy at its daily happenstance, blessing land
With its tears, the creatures of its vision . . .
Gull turning with a terribly egocentric cry,
Plumage a vicious white turning black in the etched distance;
Spore of the sun as the child is . . .

Another verse and the child mouth curves again
Into a shape swift as a dove, blue in the chilling mist;
But his heart quick as a dove's heart knows little of the cold
And has no thoughts except of love
For the dove's the latest offspring of Creation
— later than men, almost brainless,
Flies well and knows its home, is first and last the worker
Of patterns in love, the dances of love, linked beaks and sounds of
            love sewn into fabric of Time and the Earth . . .

And will he be the survivor? animicule with no anguish
Who'll watch the sun swell monstrously? unknowing
What suns are? why light becomes red?
Whose eyeballs'll become twin pygmy roses as the light becomes red?
Feathers the faint pink which'll be the white of those days?
And die in pairs singing of love
Til ice catches fragile throats?

But the child sees that terror — wings of his lips flap like
                                        crows
And his voice becomes a "KAW" . . . a want, a will
To live! His song wills it harder and his lips become a raven
Devouring intense fragments of living matter in the deadly North;
Scheming how to live becomes wiser;
Seeds the egg with wisdom, becomes wiser,
Birth by rebirth becomes wiser —
Til his firey mirthful eye sets on the sun,
Takes as into a beak its red pepper ball and his voice grown
                        terribly wise and fiercely sweet in the long ages
Calls the sun's new name and lights it again . . . !

The child sways like sapient wood in the mind — his mouth gets
                        round as an O
In mist curling away like the beard of a dying God . . . His
                        mouth's like a hollow
Nest in a swinging tree : tongue darts out
And in, out again like the red head of a nestling both fearful
                        and curious . . .
One last long note rises to High C — the cloud parts, *the
                        sky's dizzy with swallows* . . .
Til suddenly his voice breaks, sputters like an old volcano
. . . and the birds are frightened.

THE ASSASSINATION OF KENNEDY

Truthful men lack that permanent pose
, feet rooted, cocks and guns
ready to shoot right and left
as chance calls it. Liars
stand like that
but the winds we soar in
eventually rip out their roots.

I swear I feel something
of the poet's exultation,
tho lately I've been sticking my head
out a door or window
to cry

not for him or his accused killer
. . . impossible to tell exactly who for
there are so many ones . . .
tho in talking about them
I'm cold and clever.

Each morning I shave myself
with the razor of my calculations
— nicked or not, hoping
the new face in the mirror
will be innocent;

so by minute and by year
I've gained an incredible assurance
. . . maybe fating me one day to be led out
, an "*arrogant red*", smiling
in the teeth of their final lie
Death . . .

The slamming shout of a bullet
smashes sift*matter, sudden
night crashes in on a brain.

*soft

KISS

The twist, the bend or arching up
to kiss, always includes — with me
, a watching of myself. It's a stepping
into strangeness, becoming the man
of hoped-for truth, who moves in the blood.

Was it so with Judas? The step towards
the man moving in grace, the clutch
and the shape his body took, lips leading
. . . was it felt? Was the betrayal
felt as if two men, the mover and the motion
were there, balanced in the walk and the stop?

It's a ceasing to be the dry grainy self
of affairs, the bringing of another
into the arm's loop, the compass
the body contains for itself. Like
receiving a kiss, it's the new breath
of a new spirit, allowed by yours
in the presence you carry . . . and a living guess
included in your memories, hopes and urges.

A new complexion of colors. The god (the thing
out there that's the tone of kindness) comes down
for you both, into you both. Two people stand
for a wonderful one, as if it were a new person.

I'm thinking of a sudden kiss I got from
a stranger I'd been watching, and thus knew
she'd been watching me . . . in a crazy coffee house
where she used to come and go dancing
from table to table, kissing all
she acknowledged part of the company
. . . a contract to love and be loved.

Thus it'll be when the last rabbi crowns
the Messiah . . . It'll be a kiss
he's topped with, and all enraptured souls
will kiss and joyfully allow each other to exist.

106

DETAIL OF A CITYSCAPE

Have you noticed
how the cripple
struggles
onto the bus?

From where I sit
a hand,
white-knuckled
on the rail
is all I see;

and then the parts,
a head, an aimless
cane flopping,
hooked to a wrist,
levering elbows,
the poor twist
of a torso,
finally those disobedient
feet.

Once on, he lurches
onto the unrailed bench
next to the driver
. . . the most uncomfortable seat;

because if he tried for another
the surge of the bus starting
would upend him.

CROSSING THE ROCKIES

Great flowers of stone/Ambrose-bowls
For Gods whose lips are clouds writhing all with snow
Stand uncarved inside the peaks of The Rockies —
At times those mountains seem to fade into flexions of the sky
Till high cliffs and ledges look like runes broken with dynamite
Onto walls of the world, this world being a cold cave . . .

There's no shame in defeat by The Rockies;
Turning into a christmas tree on a flatcar
Which raises one bruised twig to
Write on the wind only what the wind wants not . . .

Breathe on the sky only what the sky wants not: —
Rolling in waves, invisibilities and I
Am a voice overlaid when outer space floods in as silence:
Breathe in with your life whatever life is and wants, breathe out
    changed
Whatever life is and wants
Or wants not
Yet . . .

THE CIGARETTE MACHINE

Always apart, with a row of figure-flecked
brands for eyes (How does one read surety
into a thing that never thinks: "No . . .
No cigars for sale here. Cigars don't matter!"
?) like someone who never feels lonesome
one stands, so designed that
it seems always at the moment before flight.

Only in part has thought touched; and feeling
's better described as "sense", or some word
more partial. This
is what nobody ever wanted in the way the tongue tugs back
in the word "want" : this flies so high
in the thin wind of abstraction that the eye glazes
and skids as if on its own shallow moisture
over the glitter — a dead glitter — of its surface.

At the centre of a thousand beings who think
it doesn't think, only controls
them . . . Think of the blanking of the cheeks
, sucking a cigarette, of the thousand ways
one expresses a dread detachment, a
detachment come from dread; or drooping from the lips,
a man-cancelling toughness, or bewilderment
(I've seen that); or for a matter of fact the way
the match is shaken out, tossed with one jerk
, as if it were a life calling for love.

Time's an invention, not of men, but of matter
evolving thru life toward life, of amoebae
perhaps. Cancel out time and imagine the lines
going out from each trickley clutch of change
dropped in the box : of the web entangling brands
each tasting *like any other brand . . . rotten*
; of the smoke reaching and making felt
each tube and baglet of the lung; of the spots
of purposelessly multiplying cancer; of the knife
a corny older poet might call "compassionate";
of all those rich men's sons, rich sons' fathers,
with their right hands elevated, abolishing the Hippocratic Oath
as a hypocrisy few people have the energy left
to give a damn about.

POEM WRITTEN IN A ONE-TREE FOREST

I'm sitting on the trunk-thick branch of a fir
(or something) on the Provincial Parliament lawn
    in Victoria
Smoking the best cigar I ever smoked
(Well actually I'm not . . . I *was* sitting there
And that bloody tree attracted this poem as a taller
    one might attract lightning
And I had to walk at least eight blocks to get pen and
    paper . . .
(Is anything rarer than a pen and paper in Victoria
The big petty-booj tourist centre?
— sometimes I think the middle class is all illiterate!
Anyway I have a Poetic License
($\#\sqrt{-1}$ if you want to know)
Hung around my spiritual neck on a collar made of
    genuine feeling human skin
— not very much of it left —
So allow me to tell you I'm sitting on the Provincial
    Parliamentary lawn in Victoria
On the trunk — not the root — of a fir tree *
And furthermore my feet are on the ground.

It's shady here . . . The branches are thick
And the earth under the tree is a brown rolling-hillocky
    crazy sort of a pavement
And I'm sitting (Oh Christ did I say trunk? It's a
    branch, not a trunk, not a root
Tho it's thick as a trunk of some trees and snakes
    wildlife-like over the ground as if it was a root
And is held four-to-six inches off the ground by little
    pieces of 2x8 boards painted green with very accurate
    notches cut in them and blocked up with loving
    security
And all the lower branches are like that — should of
    been dead long ago, drooped to earth and rotted:
    but they've been propped up with these boards
    (beside the tree they *do* look like boards tho properly
    I'd call them planks

*At that time I was not so keen at penetrating the many perfidious disguises of the good old Jackpine.

And I repeat the notches are very accurately done and
  the boards (I kid you not) are painted green
And since I wrote that last verse I've walked back to
  the tree
And I'm sitting on the same trunk writing in the shade
  and I see the boards were indeed once painted —
  maybe green
And it was a long time ago and those boards *were*
  indeed firmly blocked in place
With other pieces of the same material — so long ago
  that the blocks on the earth
Intended to keep the fir boughs from drooping to earth
  and rotting
Are themselves rotting — and maybe the carpenter who
  cut those accurate notches
Is dead now — and what will become of the tree?

And towards the front of the tree-shade there's a little
  garden
And forest flowers of such moist colors as would never
  live in the sun
Are growing — for this is a forest
Of one living tree and pieces of dead tree carved
  by Man
And the boards now that I notice it, are every size
  from 2x6 to 2x10
And up the side of the tree (I noticed this before was
  going to talk of it before):
THERE'S A STACK OF SWITCHBOXES! each
  bigger than the other, one above the other
And what the hell are they doing on a tree? There's
  no lights on the tree!
And from the switchboxes there is a thick cable leading
  down into the earth
Mysterious subterranean depths
And all this happened exactly as I wrote it

And now I've climbed to a higher branch of the
  tree to write what I thought in the first place
That the living tree, the dead pieces of tree used to prop
  it, the maybe-dead carpenter who helped it to survive

The flowers, and me Milt Acorn — one-time a carpenter,
      now a poet
Who people keep writing to tell him he's famous
And in fact most people never heard of
And the best cigar I ever smoked
— now puffed right down to the butt, and thrown away
— better in fact than the cigar the Cuban Ambassador
      gave me when I read him my poem about Che
      Guevara
And this poem or non-poem or whatever you might
      call it
Written just as it happened (with a lot of things left *
      out); the American tourist almost speechless from a
      stroke who I asked the way to the store left out —
      how he struggled to talk left out
This poem with all these things left out written in a
      one-tree forest
From which I look out strangely on Victoria
All these things are part of one green-and-brown-and-
      other-colors continuing movement
Growing into itself, growing out of itself,
And in-and-out motion all thru space and time with
      thoughts and feelings painting in the joints
And is the electricity in that cable so different from
      the electricity in the nerves, that move these muscles,
      that guide this pen?

AT THE COURT OF MIRACLES

In the uncurling light, relentless it is
hurting towards the roots of my passion
day by day my beauties fall into me

each wanting me a pool for a freedom. Oh the sun's my reflected eye
and I walk one upright finger tickling my bluesky God.
The children are pennies, bright
as my giving glance and tho the cars run on my loneliness
oneday soon I'll stop them all and shake hands with each driver.

*For poetic consistency, the printer left something out here. I forgot
what it was.

112

Birds are my newsboys, calling
the minutes of the just who loft their heads among them,
and the worms are tailors sewing my suit with themselves for threads.
A rose stands forever bursting and still, pink
as the inside of my eyelid, and I'm stopped unwavering
on the wavering road, living on the inward parts of a moment.

"Since there's no God . . . everything is forbidden,"
read the mottoes on the billboards. I know
the enforcers are armed, that it's a miracle I exist, that it's a miracle
I continue to be a miracle. Because I've defied them
a day opens ten thousand wings. As long as I've got one sound tooth
I'll gnaw this greenearth biscuit. No my dear demanding sirs
I will *not* turn a triple somersault thru my asshole.

THE KING RAINS

The king rains like a bloody waterspout
that gathers in the elements and spews them out
onto the noses pointing him, the upturned
pack of eyes, the brocade of the courtly city.

Truly he rains. Ask the sad hounds, worshippers
in the loaded wind, how all men rain, how every draught
bears fragments escaped from their urgencies.
Maybe this is why the dogs know better . . .

By no reflections, by no estranged energies
bouncing in their own crazy context, do they know
their gods, or for that matter their devils, but
by particles just shook loose . . . homunculi perhaps.

The king eats, and the lowly vegetable, the stupid
moo-cow flesh becomes royalty — grand gestures, surges
of vision inpainted with power . . . And out
it goes! Ah manure! That once tottered so high!

113

Gurgled from the sewers of history, the rivers bear it
to plebian seas. The clerk, paid less than a laborer,
tidies his balls' threadbare covering and still votes
conservative. Does that dirty worn string, the continuum
of his consciousness, still wave in fantastic breezes?

The king points down his beard and listens. Oh grandly
does he permit the light whose flux is the blood of souls
to illuminate even his royal planet of a heart! "I am
your friend . . . oh let my worshipful word clothe itself
in your proud and glorious body!" And the king says, *
"Friend! What does it mean? What interest of mine
can you fulfill? Which do we have in common?" "Inwardness,
outwardness . . . And the going to and fro between them,"
the councillor, if he were wise and brave, might answer

if the king were not a fool. Then he might look up
and see himself take shape in the king's eyes,
as if we all bore shields like mirrors, and the reflection *
made the object, or else our meanings
dropped sizzling into the crucibles of one another's wills.

The king's a secret heretic. "Look at my hunting pack,"
he thinks, "How well they know what men are! And what makes
        men?
My pleasure! How wrong
it is to say that I've got no dominion over souls!"

The king tells his confessor, is forgiven, feels a chilled moment
the winds of imagination blowing thru him; peasants
sowing his bones; armorers hammering out his shape.
Last night he dreamt he was a splattering pool

and his rain was a rain of bloody sweat. Splashes made rings
that ran out crisscrossing to his farthest edges. Then suddenly
some clouds — some men — would no longer rain, but stood over
        him
: shadowing. He woke up crying, "Revolution!"

He slept again and dreamt he was a spark
hissing along the fuse of time.

----

*Verse-break after line five.
*A Yankee new-left editor, stuck for copy, once put this, in garbled
form, into the mouth of a rebel student. He got the intent wrong.

114

POEM

Hair flowing yellow and still
to her shoulders, I
saw my sister once
stand before a new flower
and in a hushed voice
give it a name:

and as she cupped
her first gardenia
under her collarbone
today I held
as a vein round my heart
an unwritten poem;

a word — a few words
delicate as linked blossoms,
more delicate
being thoughts, and
only when winds start
licking them to nothing

do I write so
I may bring you my poem
to find the music of a name,
its vowel-tones to my ears
as a flower reflected in her eyes.

GHOSTLY STORY

In winter twilight on a side street,
black — touched at the edges by snow,
with secondhand cars parked headlight to trunk,
a deadeye glow in each window,
I heard a "clip-clop," "clip-clop"
ringing as if the earth was hollow.

And all white with his tall ears
dusting the underside of heaven, a Clydesdale
with mighty brushes of hair on his hooves
swelled and swept from the shadows
. . . One moment I stood in his friendly eye
then like a lord he passed me.

With all the pride of his vanished race
he switched his big wind of a tail,
then turned a corner
and his hoofbeats abruptly stilled,
leaving one steaming brown bun
and a hush as if sparrows were listening.

THE GIRL REALIZED AS BEAUTY

Always you become more real
Without ever being really;
The eternal approach
With never a touching — *

You are like the light on my table
Forever changing hairdos, hats and shades;
So whatever shape is kindly or malignant
I must judge in your spray or tints . . .

*touch

So I thought, and so I think
When all of which I say "are"
Has become "were" — you stink
In my memory, dark bee-catching flower;

Devourer of the pretty, spitter-out
Of men's just remnants like seeds;
I'm thinking of a light drizzle in the sun
Fallen through poison . . .

POEM FOR SYDNEY *

Wisdom makes us hesitant
. . . true, but
it's no wisdom that doesn't sometimes
make us bold

; or wish to be bold. No one wise
as I hope
              I am
                        could look
into the dewy country of
your smile
and not think of loving.

There are few things left for
a heart echoing like mine is
. . . the horses are gone
            , the sparrows
are rare: in this far land the robins
sound embarrassed
                        . . .

      but I love the way you sing,
   almost whispering, as if you thought aloud
among the ridges
                        of each man's or woman's
ear.

*I must confess Sydney is a woman. But it does make a nice gay
poem doesn't it? I'm heterosexual almost to the point of sexism.

117

ON THE RECURRENCE OF POETRY

(A Poem Composed During The Last Dream Of The Night)

Her voice, and then the door closes.
You close the car door, step on the gas,
Still light with her presence but
Already beginning to feel
A slight undertow of anguish
That things aren't always like that;
And already you don't know
If it'll ever happen again *

  *Yes. BRIGHTMOON was a gay poem. But I don't drive a car
either.

I'VE GONE AND STAINED WITH THE COLOR OF LOVE

I've gone and stained with the color of love
The two hundred and fifty pound road foreman
Gone on his liquor, who sits
On my wicker armchair and strains it
So much in every binding point it can't even creak.

I've known him as a laugh-cursing soldier;
I've known him posed decisively as a statue
Out on the road, telling them what to do.
I've known him so much sufficing himself
Carrying his lunchpail . . .
                    But here he sits
And his eyes are like a bull's except
A bull's eyes don't hurt and his do . . .

Or does a bull cast such a poignant hurtful look
At the slaughterer between the blow and his collapse?
I've gone and stained with the color of love
Bulls too; and this man is called Bull . . .
He says to me, "Milt — You old bastard!"
And I say, "Bull — You old bastard!"
We've told each other about all our nicknames:
But his life was this —His Childhood and The War;
And all that followed was a disappointment.

118

I've gone and stained with the color of love
Life: — Well here is a man who knows life . . .
We tell each other about our wives
His dead, mine lost, his lost before her death:
And I say, "Bull, you old bastard!"
And he says, "Milt, you old bastard!"
It being the admission of manhood
That each have done wicked things.
So we pitch arguments back and forth;
But sometimes he just sits and watches me work.

TO GAIL

Since I've come to know
That the wind's your hair
Flying over the Earth's body
Which is your body;

Flying over my body
Which is on it
(a nest upon it
with all round parts of me
even my eyes
for eggs

(my head of hair too
the weaving of that nest
so I bury myself in you - - -

You are with me;
You can't escape
Because
I can't escape you

THE NATURAL HISTORY OF ELEPHANTS

In the elephant's five-pound brain
The whole world's both table and shithouse
Where he wanders seeking viandes, exchanging great farts
For compliments. The rumble of his belly
Is like the contortions of a crumpling planetary system.
Long has he roved, his tongue longing to press the juices
From the ultimate berry, large as
But tenderer and sweeter than a watermelon;
And he leaves such signs in his wake that pygmies have fallen
And drowned in his great fragrant marshes of turds.

In the elephant's five-pound brain
The wind is diverted by the draughts of his breath,
Rivers are sweet gulps, and the ocean
After a certain distance is too deep for wading.
The earth is trivial, it has the shakes
And must be severely tested, else
It'll crumble into unsteppable clumps and scatter off
Leaving the great beast bellowing among the stars.

In the elephant's five-pound brain
Dwarves have an incredible vicious sincerity,
A persistent will to undo things. The beast cannot grasp
The convolutions of destruction, always his mind
Turns to other things — the vastness of green
And of frangibility of forest. If only once he could descend
To trivialities he'd sweep the whole earth clean of his tormentors
In one sneeze so mighty as to be observed from Mars.

In the elephant's five-pound brain
Sun and moon are the pieces in a delightfully complex ballgame
That have to do with him . . . never does he doubt
The sky has opened and rain and thunder descend
For his special ministration. He dreams of mastodons
And mammoths and still his pride beats
Like the heart of the world, he knows he could reach
To the end of space if he stood still and imagined the effort.

In the elephant's five-pound brain
Poems are composed as a silent substitute for laughter,
His thoughts while resting in the shade
Are long and solemn as novels and he knows his companions
By names differing for each quality of morning.
Noon and evening are ruminated on and each overlaid
With the taste of night. He loves his horny perambulating hide
As other tribes love their houses, and remembers
He's left flakes of skin and his smell
As a sign and permanent stamp on wherever he has been.

In the elephant's five-pound brain
The entire Oxford dictionary'ld be too small
To contain all the concepts which after all are too weighty
Each individually ever to be mentioned;
Thus of course the beast has no language
Only an eternal pondering hesitation.

In the elephant's five-pound brain
The pliable trunk's a continuous diversion
That in his great innocence he never thinks of as perverse,
The pieces of the world are handled with such a thrilling
Tenderness that all his hours
Are consummated and exhausted with love.
Not slow to mate every female bull and baby
Is blessed with a gesture grandly gracious and felt lovely
Down to the sensitive great elephant toenails.

And when his more urgent pricking member
Stabs him on its horrifying season he becomes
A blundering mass of bewilderment . . . No thought
But twenty tons of lust he fishes madly for whales
And spiders to rape them. Sperm falls in great gouts
And the whole forest is sticky, colonies of ants
Are nourished for generations on dried elephant semen.

In the elephant's five-pound brain
Death is accorded no belief and old friends
Are continually expected, patience
Is longer than the lives of glaciers and the centuries
Are rattled like toy drums. A life is planned
Like a brush-stroke on the canvas of eternity,
And the beginning of a damnation is handled
With great thought as to its middle and its end.

THE HOUSE IS GONE

A ragged curtain
And a plant in the window
Of the little house squashed hard
Against the sidewalk.

The house is gone,
Door step crazy,
Boards chewed by weather.
For a while there was a hole
And then it closed
Like an eye winking
And leaving no trace.

Once I knocked on the door
And someone answered who knew me,
Said, "Hello Milton!"
And how he said it was a surprise
Curse blunted by kindness.

The house is gone —
Let's hope they have a better one
For it stands in my thoughts with four corners
As we ought to print a period
                                                    □

APPLE-TREE IN THE WIND

Which is the sun and which is the wind
Sweeping like a yellow broom?
The shadow of my garage — called a studio
By my mother, who must confer me dignity
Creeps with its gable like a spearpoint . . .

And now its point is lost it tosses
A whole head of shadow-plumes
Borrowed from another tree;
Softened before it reaches the apple-tree —

Where the wind waves leaf-fans
Covering one red apple-face
To open another . . . Red balls
Ready to bounce into the mouths of children;
Or maybe if I'm not too lazy
Into applesauce, made by my mother:
The stove is waiting and humming: —

GO LITTLE EYES

Go little eyes and get yourselves a proper view
By being birds in it — Spill a sky from your throats
With the cloud balloons for "Gosh" "Wow" "Yeah"

Go the grassflower scented breezes, go my eyes
Set upon ants' heads, prows of fishing canoes, swinging
From charm bracelets, berry-tasting snakes' tongues —

Slide down heaven-in-a-looking-glass to star-grains-of-sugar;
Color your snow seven ways to fly
Onto my canvas and paint me hilly: —
Come you take me in like a wasp in amber
Fitted onto baby penises, jumping wallaby toes
— to tickle the wind a willow away . . .

WORDS SAID SITTING ON A ROCK SITTING ON A SAINT

(In Memoriam: Red Lane)

I

He had a way of stopping the light
, making it mark his darkness,
and a depth like a sounding line
played out, swinging its futile
weight far above bottom
, drank all his surfaces.

WARNING . . . Don't tempt the gods
with too much patience, for he poked
for poems as in the sand for stones
— round firm things, with no entrances

: and would wait for the end
of the time he was in, for
that discovery, the moment of vision
that for him was hard, like a stone

: and I reached out tendrils of thought
towards him . . . If he told me what a flower
was to him, I'd tell him what a flower
was to me. Thus we worked on each other,
patiently, as if each was immortal.

His dying is like an infinite grey sphere
of nothingness to the left hand of my sun,
and sometimes I draw the nothingness down
to wrap about me, like a cloak with a hood.

II

The saint of stone silences
is dead. The miracle is
that he does not speak,
even as when he made his sparing
moves in our game, his speakings
were flint fragments of no language,
harder silences.

The miracle is that the Earth still traces
all the circles of her whirling dance,
and those yo-yos of the sun, the comets
still comb their white curly hair
across the heavens, while he
as in life consents to all their courses.

Doomed to his time, he accepted it
and made a gnomic utterance of it. Caught on it
across, like a bow on a fiddle string
he drew the one note it was meant to say
by his agency, and concluded it
with the quietness that was its continuation.

SELF-PORTRAIT

I've got quite a face, thank God
for smiling or scowling;
tho the smile doesn't earn me much
(so knowingly innocent

and forgiving of all
they bewilderingly find themselves to be
people wonder what they've done
and edge away from me)

: but the scowl — that's different!
especially when I stick a cigar in it.
If they have any plans
for bringing me crashing down on it

They give them up. Either way
no one believes in the puddle of mother's milk
that almost floats my heart, or how
the miracle of a human being's existence

disarms me. I guess I see enough evil
as it is, without it being tossed like acid
into my eyes
— the way most people get it.

TO CONCEIVE OF TULIPS

Heartswell in the mind, presence of purple
. . . to dream of swallowing a color,
warm ice cream and peace under the navel.

My arts are the impossible shades
I see under closed eyelids, the attributes
with which I caress my friends, not the amendments
time makes as it passes, but the stillness
sudden and lasting of a brainrooted flower.

It's hardest to reconcile oneself to freedom
. . . the pain of choice, the pain
of another's choice of not you as you want yourself
but part of her own existence;
flowers are quieter; they rest
within your skull as a delicate carved bowl

: and are a tremble, a trickle, a voiceless
kindness that includes a deep light of you, a
loving consent to your life,
                              a refuge from rage.

O IN WHAT POWER

O in what power
and tenderness, whatever power
and tenderness you come
to her first time

(having come to terms with the frost
annually, having come to terms
and worked in its lands, having
gone down in the gully where the oriole tries
his voice, and added notes)

126

(having come on, come on, and
let it come, let it come
having not watered
the nettle of pride, having
touched, retreated and stood a half step back
a patience of times, and finally
melted into her melting
coming on)

, the time that's in her own terms, you having dared
to guess a swerve into her fall thru free space, O
every rose opens on its own morning, and the sun
the sun . . . . It's his first too.

POEM FOR A SINGER

Let me be the mane that swings
(clouds tossing, lightning-shot)
about the singer's muscled face,
caressing and letting it go wild.

Or let me be the oars' pulse
throbbing thru that figurehead
to the heroic Argo, that woman alive
who sang against the crash of spray

over her nipples, her chin,
and every love-wrought pore of her,
against the flattening calm, visions
washing up and down her spine.

I've tried to get that touch,
sufficient enough in myself to know
what's loved must fly its own directions
for sake of all my fantasies.

She sings and it seems to be my lips
which curl about a prisoner's curse,
I who watch while graves pop open
and the dead sing of how they've lived.

She sings in a crowded coffee shop,
smoke curling among tenuous ghosts
of the living: "Love!" she cries.
They scratch at love with palsied hands.

A pale assemblage of moons with no planet,
their mouths pluck as easily into a sneer
as to a yawn: "Sorrow!" cries the singer
. . . but their diluted tears . . .

"Courage!" cries the singer; but today
only the stupid or the very wise are brave.
"Justice!" Right now they won't be just
even to themselves, even to their souls

squirming like worms on a hook. No gods
they have but grey abstractions mulling
in the flaccid null-brain of Moloch: and
they live not by their own hopes but by his.

She sings as time and place have fated her
to people teetering on the last rung
of the last ladder down to the abyss;
who, one foot wavering down, feeling nothing

. . . feeling nothing but death for themselves,
desire the death of the entire world, because
even the imagination of life
is forbidden by all their teachers.

Let me be the song! Take me
as part of your beauty or an insult, like
a firebird above the last cloud of the last
dark planet, whose song of colored light

speeds into emptiness, creates emptiness,
transmogrifies emptiness to something like
itself, its sweet self. Oh let me be
that singer herself, with her guitar

crossed like a shield over her heart,
perched on this bomb of a world, every instant
ticking . . . ticking . . . Remembering,
remembering that she lives. Oh let me be

like the men and women of her song, those workers
who living in the very air made hideous
by the oppressor's breath, fought him
for every loose atom of their humanity. Oh let me

in these that might be the world's last days
be brave as they were, as the singer is . . . This heart
is necessary; even in the shadow
of Mount Death, it's necessary

: for the standing up proud and hopeful way, the
way expressing the truth of our lives,
we ought to die
is the only way we might live.

THE PRINCE OF CARIBS

The Prince of Caribs, in the cartoon, has a bold cloud-size talk-balloon
Blanking half the Caribbean sky, saying:
"This woman juicy black an' big as me. She mine: — "
His look drifting from hers to a cask of table wine: —

(He'd just captured a Spanish slaveship;
Given the marines an armored dip;
Laughing at the clang of sharks' teeth on iron:
Then turned a blackout eye on his Bantu woman: —

He said, "Fuck first! Eat later!"
And clicked his teeth like an alligator . . .
She never knew if he meant her for breakfast
And never dared ask —

The truth is he drew it himself: —
The truth is he learned to write too
And published a menu tenderly praising priests, especially braised
Plus calling Spanish soldiers tough at war but
Tougher in the jollity of subsequent peace
Passing from jaw to jaw in a Carib feast.

Later when he played with his chocolate boys
Often he'd click his teeth like an alligator,
Pinched muscles and grunted, "Me let'um grow a few years yet!"
Never hit a kid or a lady but
Was pretty near the under-thatch dictator . . .

All of time dreaming of the future world
As a big green salad, topped with an orange;
His clan a wandering one among tasty things on legs;
Abducting strange women, getting stranger, setting trickier
                                                    ambuscades: —

"Lucky there's no girls to get onto the trick,"
He'd often tell his cronies in the Men's Club,
"If that Old Lady got mad to pick up a stick
My flavor'd be mixed one —
                          blood and mud . . ."

Note: Due to their Christian superstitions about the resurrection of the body, leading
them to fear what would happen if they were reawakened in another man's body,
European soldiers were terrified of cannibals.
The Caribs made fright-propaganda out of this. *M.A.* *

*I forgot to add. Caribs were never cannibals.

ONE DAY KENNEDY DIED
AND SO DID
THE BIRDMAN OF ALCATRAZ

(Why was Kennedy killed?
He was a rich warmaker
who was beginning to learn
that war didn't pay —
That no people who resisted
him was helpless . . .
                    On
the day he died, murdered
no one will admit knowing
by whom —
                    Another man
who had done far more good
to the human race,
                    died;
I wrote this poem —

The world rolls,
lives flick off,
rain in the dark.
Oftener than I blink
they fall
, each one more
momentous
than a sun going out.
Shall I make fractions
of my tears? ration to each
one molecule of salt?
How many shots in Texas?
How many hungers
fade only
as the mind fades?

Yet I love Prince Charley
because he's a boy I know of
and a boy's portion is love.
Churchill's cigar, Khrushchov's shoe
are talismans I touch
vaguely with the spirit.
Unlike some friends I don't snarl
"Good riddance!" but
for each one lost I have
a particular kind of sorrow.

For Kennedy, the image-man,
his very soul wired
and tugged into shape
by advertisers, his words
so evidently sincere
and false, false, I mourn
with Sartre
for the hell that is other people
. . . the man who never was:

But for Stroud in his cell
with a roaring toilet
who just the same fashioned
a heaven of birdsongs
for himself and others,
I cry sincerely
precisely because
the assassin failed

OUR GAME

Thinking of Looey and his gestures elegant
like a chess-player (that swallow swoop
of the hand in slow motion, the piece
hooked between thumb and two fingers
, the shorter hop, and the base tilted
an instant on the square, before setting down).

I go on to how the pieces come into our game
telling of themselves in whispery thoughts
while the voices shout, and our hopeful passions
shout, "This is it . . . it!" "Yes or no!"

And Looey, who has so desperately thought
is a failure — his moves all wrong: and
perhaps I, sitting here like a pudgy
statue of "The Thinker," perhaps I
who so earnestly try to explain
what I am and am not . . . ?

Funny . . . I can't think of you as a piece.
My game — if it is a game — 's become inscrutable
and I think only of yours, just begun and
wonder what wonderment you've made of me.

See the chessman in the player's hand, looking up thrilled
, made all one drum of a pulse by the touch: saying
"I love you!" and rejoicing in the words
tho they may go all unheard. How he longs
for the melding of power and concept, that move
which'll make him transcendent!

Each of us both piece and player . . . I sign myself
With your kiss on the inside of my backbone, all given
to love which is all of eyes fixed thoughtful on us.
Oh there's Looey, and so many to help . . . so many games
all to be won: but this is our game, part of them all
, and we are given each other's.

POEM

You'll climb or fall from this moment
, from this ledge you're on, naked
between the clouds, with the peak
invisible, and the valley you came from.

But should the eagle come now, wild
to rip the muscles around your heart,
here you must defend, even find some
of the things you want to realize.

You are, and you've got to prove it . . . you are
and it's a collective of proofs, like rocks
to build a cairn with; and what if you are
in the end, not yourself, but the proofs?

NON-PRAYER

Dear old God, I'm not at odds with Thee;
I've got stronger friends
And more ferocious enemies —

If there's no God there's no atheist god either;
Nothing commands me to acts of villainy,
Nothing commands me to hate what doesn't exist . . .
And is there a rule against loving It?

PERFECT

Moments of inlet vision, moments
when the ugly world strikes
like a swung door.
All of a sudden . . .

Perfect! I blew a
smoke-ring. Never
when I try it; but
as for my life it seems a
succession of efforts
. . . gestures really

: then in the act of what's loosely called
"loving" a wave (I swear
all the cells jerk)
washes clean thru me:
or I bang my fingertip
down on the page,
"That's IT!" and take off
on rockets
in all directions

. Later I wonder
what did it? Is it the coming
together of me and a symbol
that momentarily becomes
me? a crossing of two
lines always changing
in time? or

a slit of light,
blinding, sudden, and
just for an instant
in the black bag
of another's existence

(her reflexes, her
expediences, her fumbling
love and approximations of living,
even her lies
held to with a desperation
maybe forgotten)?

Whatever it is, it's less
and more than the ideal,
which maybe is just me
and also a particularity

: but it lasts . . . for
ever and ever
I'm a boy on a swing,
winds reversing always
over the night-sky my carpet

LOVER THAT I HOPE YOU ARE

Lover that I hope you are . . . Do you need me?
For the vessel I am is like of a rare crystal
that must be full to will any giving. Only
such a choice at the same time is acceptance
as it is a demand high and arrogant.

Christ! I talk about love like a manoeuvre of
armored knights with drums and banners!
Is it for you whose least whisper against my skin
can twang me like a guitar-string? for
myself? or for something stronger than the saw
that cuts diamonds, yet is only a thought of perfection?

And this is not a guarantee, only a promise
made by one who can't judge either his weakness
or his strength . . . but must throw them
like dice, one who never intended to play
for small stakes, and who once having made the greatest gamble
and lost, lives for the next total throw.